Too Many Mothers

Roberta Taylor is one of Britain's most respected actresses. A member of the Glasgow Citizens' Company, Roberta has worked for years in theatre. In 1997 she became a household name when she played Irene Raymond in the BBC soap *EastEnders*. She now stars in ITV's *The Bill*. She lives in London.

'A marvellous book! I couldn't put it down. Roberta Taylor brings that era and that part of London zinging to life with such an authentic voice. It's so rare to find East Enders given their real voice.' Helen Mirren

'A gut-wrenching memoir that still has you gasping with laughter. I don't know of any other book that captures the stink of poverty like this and still celebrates. A hell of a book. Give it to your prosperous friends who wonder what it's all about.' Frank McCourt

'The Taylor family's mid-20th century version of East End life is discomfortingly close to Dickens's depictions of survival in the slums a century earlier. All the same there is a tremendous generosity and a good deal of dark humour in Taylor's telling of her family's story ... Reading Taylor's prose is like listening to a fascinating and feisty friend.' Melanie McGrath, *Evening Standard*

Too Many Mothers

AN EAST END CHILDHOOD

Roberta Taylor

ATLANTIC BOOKS

LONDON

First published in Great Britain in 2005 by Atlantic Books,
an imprint of Grove Atlantic Ltd.

This paperback edition published by Atlantic Books in 2006.

1 3 5 6 7 9 8 6 4 2

A CIP catalogue record for this book is available from the British Library.

ISBN: 1 84354 301 X

Designed by Nicky Barneby
Typeset in Monotype Dante by Barneby Ltd, London

Printed in Germany by Bercker
Atlantic Books
An imprint of Grove Atlantic Ltd
Ormond House
26/27 Boswell Street
London WC1N 3JZ

For Elliot, Jo and Ellis

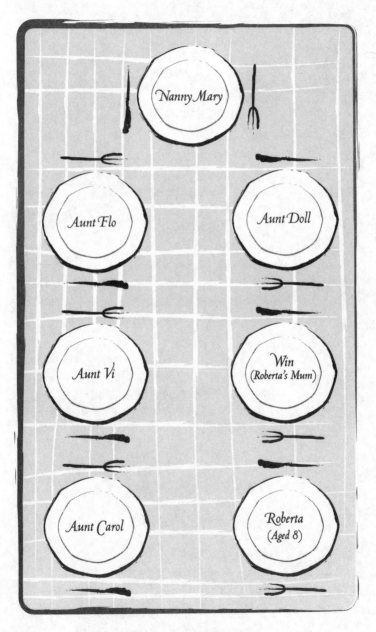

The Boxing Day Table

Boxing Day 1956

*M*ary eased her heavy legs out of bed and sat up. The room was like an icebox. Her feet fumbled around in the dark and found the torch. It was five o'clock in the morning and she had a hectic day ahead of her. The corpse that had been lying next to her gave off a fart which blew Bob into a more comfortable position. His gaping, gummy mouth closed with a damp smack. She shone the torch over the bed and grabbed one of the overcoats that masqueraded as blankets, shivered herself into it, and stared at him in the brutal pencil of light.

'His face has eaten him,' she thought, and remembered the different face and body she had married all those years ago.

CHAPTER ONE

Mary

*M*ary Roberts, née Burke, started smoking when she was nine years old, had her arms tattooed by the age of fifteen, and married my grandfather, Robert Victor Roberts, at eighteen. She shuffled the facts of her life to suit her intentions. She swore that she was born on 8 August 1900 to an Irish tinker family. Her birthday was always celebrated on the eighth of August, even though her birth certificate insists that she poked her nose into the world on 13 May 1900. Like a brass band on a Sunday morning the speed and energy of the cockney accent cooked very nicely thank you with the southern Irish tones and vernacular of her parents. The scenic route of her life would not have much to do with geography; she lived and died in the East End of London.

Mary sauntered away from her family home, away from the slums of Poplar, without so much as a by-your-leave, in February 1918, and walked four grim miles east to Bob Roberts's mother's house in West Ham. She was pregnant. How and where Mary met Bob had never cropped up. He came from a better class of cockney, apparently. Perhaps they washed more often, had antimacassars, books, and sat at the table to eat. Mary's children were in no doubt that it was the Roberts side that was the civilized side.

*

Would he marry her? Of course he would. She was gorgeous. Pale skin, green eyes, a mass of complicated red hair, and a cheeky little figure with a temperament to match. A Shetland pony in human form.

They whispered their dilemma in the privacy of Clara Roberts's front parlour.

He couldn't marry her right at that moment, he had to return to sea in two days' time. She hadn't reckoned on his going away so soon, and neither had he, but there was a war on and the Merchant Navy had an important job to do.

If Bob and his brother William managed to survive, they would be away until Christmas at least.

'In this situation, it's all hands on deck,' he tried to explain to her.

All she owned she stood up in. She didn't look that much different from most poor girls of the time, but for her hair, her swagger, and the minx-eyed look she'd give instead of a straight answer. Leaving her, Bob braced himself and walked to the scullery.

His mother and brother took the news better than they might have done in peacetime. Clara had bigger things to fret about now. Her boys were going away and she couldn't guarantee she would ever see them again.

Today was Mary's first meeting with Clara and William, and her first meeting with the inside of their house. She had sidled past a couple of times last year, out of curiosity, when she had been waiting to meet Bob at the street corner.

Her own living arrangements had consisted of a bug-infested tenement, surrounded by thieves and vagabonds. The daffy of fourteen Burkes shared one and a half rooms, one cold tap and a black cauldron on the open fire stewing lumpish, watery broth. An iron double bed catered for her mum, dad, and the three youngest toddlers. Two large mattresses on the floor slept the nine other Burkes: girls in one, boys in the other. She had slept with somebody else's feet in her face all her life.

Here, she was in a real house. Mary sniffed her future in the beeswax of the parlour. On the mantelshelf were two postcards with camels on them, a wooden-framed photograph of Bob and William in matching dark overcoats, a pair of pewter candlesticks, and a small metal candle-snuffer. The shelves on the wall to the left of the fireplace were home to a pink flowery tea set, the six cups, face down in their saucers to keep out the dust, separated by the round fat teapot. On the top shelf, taking pride of place, she eyed up an ancient-looking carved ornament of a withered old man.

She ran her fingers over the highly polished sideboard against the opposite wall and looked at the squat wooden clock sitting on a lace runner.

Three o'clock in the afternoon.

Thursday, 28 February 1918, she reminded herself.

Stealthily she opened the sideboard drawers. In the left-hand drawer, packed to the gunwales, lived pieces of yellowing lace and neatly folded gentlemen's handkerchiefs. The right-hand drawer contained a pile of formal-looking documents, a pair of scissors, some buff envelopes, and half a dozen collar studs. Right at the back of the drawer she spotted something else. A roll of large white five-pound notes gripped by a rubber band.

At the sound of the Roberts family coming towards her Mary quickly re-arranged herself as a scrap of humanity that only the coldest heart could ignore. The money stayed in the drawer. Clara was first in, followed immediately by her two sons. William had his arm around his younger brother's shoulder. It looked as if Bob had been crying.

Boxing Day 1956

'*I*, Mary Burke, a very, very bad Catholic, take thee Bob Roberts, my religious Protestant ... I even married you in your Proddy church didn't I?'

Mary left him to his slumber.

It had not been a restful night for her. She had floated between the dead and the living, in that fitful, pointless kind of sleep. Footsteps across her ceiling all night, quietening down babies and toddlers, had made her ratty.

She hadn't dreamt of the Chinaman in donkey's years.

Mary's children: between 1918 and 1943 she had laid her seven eggs. She could have laid more if she'd persevered. I am the epilogue of her life. Her granddaughter.

CHAPTER TWO

Mary

Mary never went home again. And no one came looking for her.

Tea was brought in by William, Clara held her hand and lowered her into the armchair, and Bob rolled her a smoke. Clara told her what they had decided would be for the best, for all their sakes. If she agreed, of course.

She more than did.

Mary stuck to her story, that her parents had thrown her out. No, there was nothing to go back there for. It was time for the grand tour.

Between the parlour at the front and the scullery out the back was Clara's bedroom. She would sleep here with Clara for the next two days, until the boys had gone off to sea. Mary had never seen a bed so clean, so squishy. Four large white pillows with lace edging sat like sentries on top of blankets over blankets over more blankets, topped with a shiny golden fattipuff eiderdown. There was more than enough room for the two of them; she thought of the absolute luxury of all that bed for one person. Clara hadn't shared her bed for ten years. The polished lino had green woolly runners on either side of the bed to keep your feet warm when you got up. The room was almost identical in shape to the parlour, with an identical fireplace. In the alcove stood a wardrobe with a full-length mirror for a door. The other furniture was a small round table by the window and a straight-backed wooden chair with a rattan seat by the fireplace. The fire was neatly laid but not yet lit. She peeked out of the big square window and saw that it looked onto the backyard. The six shirts and two towels on the washing line were stiff with the cold.

Mary was delicately manoeuvred into the back room to be shown the stove, the big butler-sink with its bleached wooden draining board, and the pots and pans. Something hearty was simmering slowly in a big pot on the gas, warming the whole room. Under the window was a white enamel-topped table and four chairs; an open carton of salt sat in the middle of it. They didn't bother to take Mary into the yard, just pointed to the privy and asked if she needed to use it. She didn't. It was too cold to go outside unless really necessary.

The upstairs didn't seem to match the downstairs in size. It was up here that Clara explained what was going to happen. Once the boys had left, William's bedroom would become Mary's scullery, and his bed would be moved down into Clara's room. A sink and a stove would be put upstairs, and Bob's room would become their marital bedroom. Each bedroom had a small iron fireplace, so it wouldn't get too cold. Lugging the coal up would be a bit of a hike, but they all decided it was manageable, even for a girl.

Mary gave off a dazed look while all this was going on, disguising her fleetness of tongue and brain. She looked pliable. How else could an innocent, unmarried girl get pregnant? So pliable, in fact, she allowed herself to be bathed in the zinc bath which had been dragged in from the yard, and she even let Clara unpin her hair and search for nits. Clara found none. While all this female cleansing was going on, William and Bob were placed in the front parlour.

With sterilized hair and body, she was given a set of Clara's undergarments and a long grey skirt with matching top. She was allowed to keep her own boots, for now. The women were almost the same size, except that Mary was about two inches taller. The long skirt was not as long as it should have been. She plaited her damp hair into two braids. It would dry with a pretty kink in it and by tomorrow morning appear curlier than it really was. Everything Mary had arrived in was put on the fire in the front parlour, rag by rag, and burnt. She had shed her old skin, and was preparing a new, thicker one for the future.

After supper of lamb and potato stew, she helped Clara with the washing up in the scullery while William and Bob organized the bedtime fire in Clara's room and hot-water bottles for themselves. Bob's hot glances pierced the back of Mary's neck, she felt his arm brush by her breasts to get to the tap. She never looked at him, never said a word to him.

The comfort of the fire, the armchair, and the hot milk made her eyelids and head droop as she sat in the parlour with her new family. They had all been talking about what was going to happen tomorrow. She drifted in and out, thinking of those fivers in the drawer right next to her.

Bob was given permission to walk her into the bedroom, kiss her goodnight, and put her to bed. One of his mother's night-dresses was waiting for her, laid out on the golden eiderdown. As he soaked up her lovely perfume of carbolic, Mary gave him a tired wink, a little kiss on the mouth, and sent him on his way.

Her last gasp of energy was spent taking off one set of new clothes and donning another. She took her time getting into bed. Mary wanted to luxuriate in every limb being embraced by the sharp prick of the cold linen sheets, followed by the cosy comforting weight of all those blankets. Then she conked out. She dreamt she was flying on a huge five-pound note, a magic carpet riding the breeze across the continents of the world.

The next day brought a trip to Stratford Broadway on the electric tram. William paid the fares. The Broadway was dominated by Boardman's, the fancy outfitters: three vast floors of clothing for every occasion. Bob and William went off for a stroll round the shop, while Clara fitted Mary out with a warm grey coat, two frocks, and a pair of ladies' buttoned boots. The frocks and coat were as shapeless as they could find, to make room for her pregnancy. Next stop was the underwear department, where two of everything was needed for Mary and, Clara said, 'to kill two birds with one stone', some underwear for the boys.

Wrapping up this new clobber took for ever. The old boy behind the counter meticulously cut off the individual labels, folded each garment carefully onto brown paper, and made little parcels which he tied up with string. Bob and William occupied themselves chatting to him about the state of the war, the torpedoing of a hospital ship on its way to Brest two days before, and their own imminent departure on Sunday. This was too much for Clara, so she went and sat on a chair by the entrance: the chair for weary or aged customers. Mary stood by her side, silently eyeing up the business going on at the counter. The clerk's dandruff had showered his well-worn three-piece suit; his long fingernails were grubby from ink and string. Her first new clothes. No one's else's hand-me-downs any more.

Clara twittered, 'I wish they would get a move on, I'm more than peckish now. How you doing, Mary? Starving, I'm sure. We are going to have to fatten you up, young lady.'

Mary 'mmm'-ed in agreement, through tightly clamped lips. She was staring at the backs of the two brothers. They didn't look like brothers. Where Bob was dark, delicately built, handsome, and open-faced, William was thick-set, taller, with light, colourless hair and dull yellow skin. He didn't have Bob's aquiline nose, high cheekbones, and square lips; he was not handsome at all. William was hidden in his skin. There was no light shining from him, everything was pasted down. Bob looked like his mother. Mary decided that William must take after the dead father. She eagle-eyed the payment. The brothers shared the cost. Replicas of what she had seen in the sideboard yesterday emerged from both their pockets. They counted the money out and handed it to the scurf-laden old clerk, who placed it into a tin canister along with their bill.

She watched the tin bullet fly along wires above the counter to the payment cubicle at the end of the store. A hawk-nosed spinster with a severe middle parting tallied everything up and sent the change flying back to the clerk.

'Slow down, Mary, no one's going to pinch it. At least try and taste it before you swallow it.' Bob grabbed her wrist and winked. She winked back.

Mary had almost polished off her double pie and mash, swimming in delicious green liquor, before the rest of them had even got going. Clara didn't care for the secret ingredients of the pies and had gone for her usual, jellied eels, from which she was delicately picking the bones. Mary wanted the eels as well, but knew the pies would fill her stomach for longer.

'Sorry. Am I showing you up? I've never been looked after like this before, it's made me starving hungry.' Mary studied all three of them.

'You're hungry because you're carrying,' said Clara. She said it in such a way that Mary couldn't fathom which way it was intended. It wasn't whispered or declared with any attitude, just said – as if the dustcart or the milkman had arrived, and Clara carried on filleting her food.

Mary knew she would have to keep her wits about her if she was ever going to translate the whys and wherefores of Clara's and William's thoughts.

Clara took her time, still eating long after the other three had well finished. The pie shop was getting very busy and the counter queue now stretched into the street. Some people were taking their food away with them, the rest squeezing themselves into any spaces left at the long tables, giving miserable grunts to anyone still taking up a seat after they had finished their food. Which, of course, meant Mary, William, and Bob. Mary was dying for a smoke and gestured at Bob, putting two closed fingers to her mouth and gently inhaling. He gave a shake of his head. Outside, while they waited for the tram, he whispered to her that it looked common for women to smoke in public, and he didn't want to aggravate his mother and brother. She laughed. Clara and William gave her a sharp look and shuffled their feet into different arangements.

'Fuck me, maybe even laughing makes a girl look common around this lot,' thought Mary.

Bob put his arm around her shoulder and whispered to her again, 'Soon as we're back indoors, I'll roll you one. Promise.'

Bob paid their fares this time, and Clara spent the journey talking about what they would have for their tea.

'If it's all right with you, Mary, I thought we'd have the leftover stew as soup with some bread and dripping; the lamb's all finished.' This was said as if there were some choice in the matter, yet delivered as a foregone conclusion. Not that Mary felt the need for a choice; she was getting to grips with the luxury of having two bellyfuls in one day.

She got her smoke. Bob lit the fire in the parlour, William made a pot of tea, and Clara went for a lie-down on her bed. Mary felt a bit at sixes and sevens. This domestic palaver was confusing her: she didn't quite know how to help, or when. Sweet William finished his tea, picked up the newspaper, and retired to the outside lavatory. At last they were on their own.

'Bob, you do all like me, don't you? I mean, I would help more, but I don't know what I'm supposed to do. How do you think it's going to work out? Me being here on my own with your mum?'

Bob picked her up and plonked her on his lap. He squeezed

her as tight as he could, kissed her forehead, kissed her chin, her nose, and then her mouth. She snuggled into him and wondered if she could have told him what was on her mind in a clearer fashion. She wasn't that sure herself what it was that she needed to know.

'Mum will show you the ropes. Don't worry. You can't learn what to do all in one day, can you? By the time I'm back home you'll be doing all right. Why don't you start by putting on one of your new frocks, and chuck those bloody old boots away. Come on, let's see you looking all fancy pants.'

But she couldn't. The packages were in the bedroom and she didn't want to disturb Clara.

'I'll start my fancy-pants life tomorrow. I'll get all togged up for you then.'

Tomorrow would be Saturday, their last day together. On Sunday morning at the crack, Bob and William would be off for at least six months. Mary took it for granted they would return fine and dandy. The war hadn't filtered through to her much, it was simply another aggravation to put up with. For most of the time she forgot about it.

After soup and dripping, the four of them sat round the fire, occasionally chipping in bits of conversation. Mostly it was quiet. Clara sat in one armchair darning socks, William in the opposite one knitting something grey and chunky on big fat needles. Bob and Mary were doing a wooden jigsaw puzzle of an old sailing ship on the dining table by the window. Every time one of them managed to put a piece in its right place they would tap twice on the table. 'Dah, dah!'

Bob was better at it than Mary. He knew all about ships, from one end to the other, and was concentrating. Mary was concentrating on other things. Her mind was on tomorrow, and the next day, and the next. It was draughty by the window and she wanted to get into that bed again, to be asleep before Clara came in. She was full of food and thoughts and needed to be on her own for a while.

Tomorrow morning she was going to be shown the local shops. In new frock and boots.

A spindly box shrub struggled to grow behind the low brick wall that led up the path to the front door. Number fifty was in the middle of the terrace of identical yellowy brick houses. They each had a large protruding bay window on the ground floor and two arched windows above. The windows and doors of every house had been painted in the same high-gloss brown. Clara was very proud of the fact that her windows stood out from the others. She had heavy wooden venetian blinds to protect the full-length lace curtains behind. The other houses only had lace curtains in the bottom halves of the windows, to keep out passing nosy parkers.

These streets of terraces fanned out to the high road with its small cluster of shops, a ten-minute walk away. The butcher, the baker, the greengrocer, the cobbler, the public steam laundry, the pawnbroker, and, above the pawnbroker, the herbalist. The milkman with his horse-drawn cart came very early each morning. The horse was called Plimsoll because, like a slave, he had been named after his boss, Stanley Plimsoll. Both horse and man had bad teeth, bad breath, and a bad temper. Clara took Mary into every shop – even the pawnbroker's, to climb the stairs to the herbalist above, where a paper screw of senna pods was purchased. Next stop was the cobbler's, to have William's and Bob's shoes repaired while they were away, and then on to the butcher, the baker, and the greengrocer's. This last supper was going to be as special as wartime conditions would allow, aided and abetted by little extras from the shopkeepers. Steamed meat pudding, carrots, and turnips, followed by bread pudding.

Boxing Day 1956

We were all wearing our overcoats to keep warm. 'This is a bitter Christmas,' Mum had said yesterday.

Marching from the front room into the bedroom, then back out into the passage, Nanny and Granddad were attacking each other with vicious words. I think my mum was trying to keep out of their way. She was in the scullery making tea and toast for anyone who could face breakfast after the night before, trying to keep my baby brother quiet at the same time. My newish dad was out there with her, splashing about, having a shave before someone else commandeered the sink.

I crawled into the sideboard to get away from the noise, the cold, and the horrible stink. Granddad's final performance before he had gone to bed was to spew up in the fireplace. The smell of beery sick from the grate mingled with the burning of white crusty bread floating down the passage from the scullery. My cousin, Pattie, was given the gut-tugging job of cleaning out the grate and getting the fire going, sharpish. I should have been giving her a hand, twisting old newspapers into plaits thick enough to work as kindling, or bringing in more coal from the scary outside coal-hole opposite the front door. Instead, I stayed in my sideboard, lying on the plastic-wrapped sheets that Nanny hadn't managed to peddle before Christmas – she'd been relying on the money, that's what I'd heard her tell my mum.

'What are you doing in there? They won't be in there, you silly little cow.' Nanny dragged me out and closed the door on her tallyman secrets. She gave me a wink and a 'shush' with a finger to her mouth.

Pattie was going to get into trouble as well, because she was taking so long to make the fire, using newspaper to protect her hands from Granddad's throw-up and trying to hold her nose at the same time.

'For Christ's sake, it's not going to bite you; uglier things than that have married your mother. Now get a move on, we need to get the babies fed and watered,' Nanny shouted at her.

Pattie jumped out of her skin, hitting her head on the mantel-shelf. And there they were, sitting in the middle of Nanny's frayed, rose-patterned carpet, surrounded by crumbs of last night's fire. Nanny spotted them straight away and laughed and shouted out at the same time. 'Oi, you lot, we've found them. You'll never in your pip believe where.'

Mum came running in with Buster on her hip and the grill pan in her hand. My dad followed her, half his face covered in shaving soap. I crawled back into the sideboard and peered out. Sooty lumplets of burnt coal and blackened strips of newspaper had been chucked across the floor. It was as if a chopped-off head had been burnt to ashes, the skin, bone, eyes, and mouth crushed to powder. Only the teeth were left. Teeth, I knew, were very difficult to get rid of, because the police were always searching for murdered people's dental records. The top set snarled up at us from the carpet, the lower set looking lonely and scared near the window.

Granddad's false teeth had been found at last.

'A quick brush-up and a soak in bleach for an hour and they'll be as right as rain,' Nanny said, as she picked them up and went off to the scullery.

Granddad's face would stop looking like an empty envelope

and he would be able to chew his Boxing Day Feast properly along with the rest of us.

Well almost all of us.

CHAPTER THREE

Mary

*T*he stove was in, the sink was in. Mary was in. William's bed and chest of drawers were out, downstairs in Clara's bedroom.

That last Sunday morning had seen clinging squeezes and tears between Clara, William, and Bob. They read each other's eyes for a sign that they would see each other again. It was the same at every leaving; they would never get used to it. But Mary's imagination was more stunted: she couldn't think beyond a day at a time. She heard him say he would write to her, send her money, be back in a few months. Hopefully before the baby was born. Then they would get married. That's what she heard, so that's what she accepted.

Bob was grateful for Mary's innocence, that she didn't make a fuss, and with a hug and a wave he and William strutted down the street back to some bastard's war.

It didn't take long to dawn on Clara that Mary had to be house-trained. How to shop, how to cook, how to clean.

Mary would never fall in love with hygiene or housework. All this constant washing and ironing, washing up after every meal, after every cup of tea, was such a waste of time. In the months that Bob was away Clara taught her all his favourites. Mary learnt how to make meat pudding, rice pudding, and of course, bread pudding. She was turning into a little pudding herself, the only giveaway that she was pregnant.

Pregnancy hadn't brought any new fancies or changes of mood. She was waiting to deliver a parcel, that was that.

In that first month that Bob had gone, she hadn't touched a halfpenny of the big white five-pound note he had given her. It was for emergencies, he'd said, and, nearer the time, to buy the necessary bits for the baby. The money never left her. At night it went under her pillow and during the day she walked around on it, in one of her boots. The bundle of fivers in the sideboard drawer had long disappeared. It was one of the first things she had checked out. She decided it must have been used up that day at Boardman's. Clara held the purse strings, and if Mary needed anything she had to ask her for it. A few pennies for tobacco always came with a lecture, which was getting on her nerves. That five-pound note would have to be broken into.

Mary wanted the moment; she couldn't afford the future. All her life she could deal only with the moment.

Bob had never stopped thinking about her and wrote as often as the mail and the war allowed. Mary had almost forgotten what he looked like, sounded like, or even who he was any more. There was no point in writing back, he could be anywhere.

The moment the pregnancy started to show, she made another dent in the fiver and treated herself to a cheap wedding band. By June, her breasts and seven-months-gone stomach were pushing hard at the seams of her frock. The neighbours knew she wasn't married yet but turned a blind eye for Clara's sake.

Mary's playtime came during Clara's regular-as-clockwork afternoon snooze. On bad weather days she would poke around the house, trying to find any secrets lurking there; on good weather days she would stroll through the park or to the shops, and occasionally hop on a tram.

★

How Mary got away with it she never knew. She had walked right past them before the penny dropped. That old familiar sound. The cross fertilization of two tutti-frutti planets. It was her big brother Patrick, strolling along with four other navvies, filthy dirty and laughing their heads off. It was his laughter, the way he tossed his head back, that had made him miss the sight of her, his little sister, very pregnant and looking like she had come up a few inches in the world. She heard the men stop and in that instant she was round the next corner crouching in someone's front porch. The burden of the baby made her legs and back hurt. It was time for a sit down and a smoke. 'At least eight more fucking weeks of this,' Mary moaned to herself.

She shouldn't have come here today. What was *he* doing in Stratford anyway? If the Burkes ever found her, she would lose everything. Like locusts, they would nibble every penny away, then they would start on Clara, Bob, and William until every one of them went down the sewer. She knew all their tricks; they had educated her well. Bob wouldn't stand a chance against them.

'You're as white as a sheet, Mary. What's happened? You all right?' Clara was up and busy ironing by the time Mary got back home.

'Yeah, yeah, I'm just a bit tired. I'm going to have a little kip, if you don't mind, Clara.' Mary puffed her way up to her quarters and couldn't wait to flop down on the irresistible pillows, linen sheets, and blankets. She would shroud herself in good linen for the rest of her life.

The next day Clara took Mary to the herbalist's to let him give her the once-over and check that everything was as it should be. A tonic was prescribed, or, as Mary called it, her 'bottle of jollop'. For the next weeks she didn't stray very far; she was too big to be seen in public now. To display a body that had obviously seen sexual action wasn't decent.

Eventually a slow daughter crawled out of Mary in the middle of the night, at the beginning of September 1918. Mary named her Florence Maud, after no one in particular: baby Flo.

Three days before Christmas 1918, Bob and William came back home safe and sound. They peered at the three-month-old bundle, 'umm'-ed and 'ah'-ed, asked if she was always that quiet, and plonked a red fez on her head. The hat fell over the baby's face and down to her neck. Three-month-old Flo tilted her head to one side and stayed very still. She didn't cry or panic, but simply let it all happen – a bird in a cage with its cover on for the night.

The wedding would get done in the new year. In the meantime, Clara was so bewitched with her boys being home that she allowed Bob and Mary to live upstairs as man and wife immediately. Their single bed would be replaced with a double after the wedding. She didn't want them to be too comfortable, too soon.

They were all going to have a grand Christmas.

William accepted his new arrangements, sleeping downstairs in his mother's room, with good grace. He didn't think it would be for long.

The wedding finally took place at St Luke's Church, West Ham, in March 1919. They left their seven-month-old daughter outside in her pram. The whole performance didn't take long. There was no delicate trawl down the aisle, more a quick trot to get it over and done with. The handful of witnesses consisted of Mary's future mother-in-law, future brother-in-law, two of Bob's schoolmates, and the vicar. No other Burke in evidence. She thought of letting her family know that she had come up in the world, but never got round to it. No point in sending them a letter either, because Mr and Mrs Burke and the rest of their tribe had never learned to read and write. That had always been Mary's job. And her special gift.

Boxing Day 1956

'Win, me and your dad are getting out of your way. Tell Len when he gets here that we're in the Red Lion,' my dad shouted upstairs. Mum heard him but couldn't be bothered to answer over the din. She was upstairs changing my brother Lionel, who was crying. He was exactly three months and one day old – his first Christmas on this earth. Jumping and hollering with them was my other brother, Buster Bill.

Buster Bill from Shooter's Hill. I don't know where that came from; we never had anything to do with Shooter's Hill, we just used to sing it to him when he was being good.

He was two years old and 'a fucking genius', my dad told everyone.

Nanny was in the passage, telling them not to come back pissed if they didn't want their dinner chucked over their bonces.

'Mary, you're all woman, you are,' Dad said to her.

A spanking on the door knocker made more commotion. I slid into the passage and saw that it was Aunt Doll and Uncle Len, with my cousins, Ron and Barbara.

'Perfect timing mate. Me and Bob are just off down the pub. Keep your coat on and turn round. Hiya, Doll, see you later.' Dad gave her a quick peck on her cheek, ruffled the heads of Barbara and Ron, and pushed Uncle Len and Granddad out of the door.

Aunt Doll stared at Granddad's sunken face. 'You're not going out like that, Dad, are you?' she said. 'Put your teeth in, for Christ's sake.'

'He can't, the silly old bastard. We've had a right performance here this morning,' Nanny shouted as she walked down the passage.

The door slammed and the men were out and free for a few hours.

'Kids, go in the front room and keep warm. Behave yourselves or you'll have me to answer to. Follow me, Doll, I've got to get this joint in, else we'll never get any grub.' Six-year-old Barbara and eleven-year-old Ron did as they were told. I was still half in the room and half out in the passage, and Aunt Doll gave me a peck on the cheek.

'Where is everybody?', she said as she poked her nose into the front room and then carried on towards the scullery.

I nodded my hellos to Barbara and Ron, and said I'd be back in a minute. I could hear Barbara moaning already about how cold it was.

'Win's upstairs, seeing to her two. I've not heard a peep out of our Carol and the Galoot. They must still be soundo. I don't reckon they've had much kip either. Her kids have been cantankerous all night, and that woke up Win's boys. To tell you the truth, I was grateful to be down here away from it all.' Nanny unwrapped a large leg of lamb from its bloodied newspaper as she rattled on. I hoped she was going to wash it before putting it in the oven, and from the look on Aunt Doll's face she was thinking the same thing. It had been living in its newspaper outside the back door for two days in a wooden-framed box with a chicken-wire door. It was frozen stiff. Nanny lit the oven, took out her big baking tin, and put it on the bath.

Granddad had put the bath in himself. It was opposite the stove, under the window that looked out onto the backyard.

The taps didn't work. The bath was covered in a seen-much-better-days white sheet, and on top of that he had made a worktop out of an old door. King Edward potatoes, Brussels sprouts, and parsnips were spread out, ready and waiting for peeling. The worktop was so low it was going to turn whoever got that job into a hunchback.

'Mum, give it here. I'll wash the meat and you can start peeling.'

'Fuck off, I'm leaving that job for our Flo when she finally decides to make an appearance. She had one of her turns last night and it's taken the wind out of her sails. But she's not staying in bed all day, that's for sure, I've got too much to do,' Nanny clacked as she took the glass with Granddad's teeth out of Aunt Doll's way, and lit herself a Wild Woodbine.

From the third step of the stairs I could see everything, and I could press myself into the wall. Aunt Doll had put the leg of lamb in the sink on a plate and was trying to clean off the frozen blood with the ice-cold water as carefully as she could, so as not to get her light grey, woollen duster coat spattered.

'That's a lovely coat, Doll. How much was that?' asked Nanny, puffing away and staring at the coat.

'It was a treat from our Len. I never asked. If he sees me doing this in it he'll go spare.' Aunt Doll concentrated on cleaning the meat and avoided Nanny's eyes. Money talk was dangerous talk, that's what Mum always said.

'No, it's just that I could probably have got you one. I might have saved him a few bob. Where did he get it from, do you know? I'm sure my tallyman had something very similar.' All this was interrupted by me nearly being knocked off my perch and Nanny getting a headbutt in the legs from Buster. Mum followed behind, breastfeeding Lionel.

'Hello, Doll. She put you to work already? You've not even taken your coat off. Mind you, neither have the rest of us yet.' I knew Mum was pleased to see Doll; she went over and kissed her sister straight away. Aunt Doll kissed the top of the baby's head and Mum's cheek. Buster was trying to climb on top of the worktop and play about with the vegetables.

'What's happening upstairs, Win? Any movement from anybody? . . . Don't do that Buster. Go on, go in the front room with the others.' She was taking the turnips from him with one hand and puffing her fag with the other.

'Yes, they're all awake apart from Flo. Carol and Tony are staying up there with the kids, keeping warm round the electric fire . . . Buster? Buster? Look at Mummy. Where's Robbie, eh? Go and find Robbie. Go on, call her.' Mum got his attention; he peered down the passage, looked back at her, and ran on wobbly legs towards the front room and the sound of Ron and Barbara whispering. He didn't notice me sitting on the stairs.

Lionel had fed enough and fallen asleep. Mum gave a 'thank goodness' look, did the buttons of her dress and coat up, and took him to the back room to put him on Nanny and Granddad's bed. I hoped he'd sleep for the next couple of hours. Just as the three of them were asking, 'Where's our Vi and her tribe got to?' there was a heavy double rap on the front door.

I got to the door seconds before anyone else could. My two black cousins scooted past me into the front room. Aunt Vi kissed and stroked everybody and Uncle Korim smiled shyly and wobbled his head in his funny Indian greeting. Everyone who was going to eat with us that day had arrived, except for Big George. He might or might not remember to turn up for his dinner. Big George was my favourite.

Uncle Korim was ordered to join the rest of the dads down the pub. Nanny told him not to take any notice of that miserable bastard barman, he'd be all right with the others there to look after him. He didn't look that sure about it to me.

The meat was in the oven and the vegetables were brought

into the warmth of the front room for scraping. Aunt Doll and Mum said they didn't much fancy the idea of Aunt Flo messing about with their food. Aunt Flo was frightened of water apparently.

Buster had found a corner out of the way where no one could see him pulling off the wallpaper, which meant that, as far as I was concerned, he was occupied and I could play rummy with my cousins. We argued over who was going to be in whose team for ages. Pattie, Aunt Flo's daughter, was the eldest – she was already thirteen – so she was allowed to pick the teams. I was eight so I went with Aunt Doll's Barbara who was only six. Aunt Doll's Ron and Aunt Vi's George, who were both eleven and a half, made another team. Pattie found herself lumbered with six-year-old Black Gary. He was black and glossy, and she was as white and flat as a piece of paper. We quarrelled in whispers so that the grown-ups might forget we were there. I could see Buster licking his bits of ripped wallpaper and trying to stick some of it back on.

Aunt Flo had finally got up and she came and asked if there was anything she could do to help. Aunt Doll was the only one who greeted her with a kiss. Nanny, Mum, and Aunt Vi just nodded without even looking up.

'You can put the kettle on and make us a brew,' Nanny ordered. Aunt Flo slid off down the passage. She always reminded me of Lettuce Leaf out of the *Beano*.

Nanny Mary, smelling of cabbage and cigarettes, always looked the same. She wasn't fat, but like a little wall – and so was her face, wide and strong with green eyes, scary flaring nostrils, and her mouth turned down in the shape of an 'n'. Last week's short, grey, wavy hair had been home-dyed a rusty brown for Christmas. Her voice was like laughing and shouting at the same time.

I liked my nan.

Aunt Flo, 'with the plate in her head', was tall, pale, and flat-bodied. A voiceless voice. She smelt of sour milk, had eggy, watery eyes, and lank hair scurfed back with a hairgrip. Pillow feathers sprouted out of her jumper and cardigan as if she had slept in them. She brought the tea in, cup by cup. She was a bit nervous about having both hands full at the same time.

I never really spoke to her.

Aunt Doll smelt of talcum powder. She was beautiful, even though she was fatter than the others. She had green naughty eyes and short red wavy hair like Nanny's. Now that the grey duster coat had been carefully folded over the back of her chair, you could see that her underneath was just as smart. She had the best legs of all of them and always wore stockings with a fancy patterned seam up the back.

I wanted Aunt Doll to want me.

Aunt Vi looked older than Aunt Doll. She was thin and bird-like and smelt of curry. She had a face like a knife. Her green eyes glinted with taking the piss. We had forgotten what Aunt Vi's real hair colour had ever been. For Christmas she had gone from blue-black to a custard blonde. Her skin was the colour of old newspaper. She had a mouth so small and thin that if she ever stopped speaking it would probably heal up. Her black astrakhan curly-wurly coat with the Chinese-patterned lining had been carefully placed on the bed in the other room, where Lionel was still fast asleep.

I wanted to make Aunt Vi laugh.

Next in line: Win, my mother.

I looked at her white, white skin and then down at my own mottled blue and pink skin. At her shiny black hair. I twisted my plait round to my nose to search for any black bits of my own, but found only red and brown, mostly brown. Her chocolate eyes were big and tight-skinned; mine were muddy-coloured, puffy, and small. She smelt of Lifebuoy soap. I didn't smell of anything. I clicked my eyes and photographed her for ever in that instant, while cousin Ron dealt out a new game of rummy. Her skinny body made her look taller than the others; her back was broader, her arms were longer, her feet were bigger. Her feet were famous. My face was round and podgy, my nose was short and fleshy. Why couldn't I look like her, with her straight grown-up nose, high cheekbones, and strong chin? Too strong, Mum always thought. She had the fattest mouth of all of them. I didn't even have that. Mine was the exact same shape, but shorter and narrower; both our mouths had been drawn on with a heavy pencil, and I had the same sharp points on my top lip. Maybe I would grow into my mouth.

I wanted my mum to be happy.

Nanny had spotted what Buster was up to. He was surrounded by snotty bits of her wallpaper, and her hollering and shouting stopped our game in its tracks. Pattie made herself scarce and the rest of the cousins flew out into the passage to share a sneaky fag and play for money. I had to get Buster on his po, hope for a result, clean him up, then occupy him. He was having none of it. He bounced himself onto Mum's lap, grabbed her thumb, and put it in his mouth. The po stayed near by, just in case. Pattie came back with the coal, stoked the fire, and sat staring into it. I sat in the other corner of the hearth with my colouring book and crayons on my lap.

'He might be no effing good, Vi, but he's not as dangerous as Churchill was.' Aunt Doll seemed to know what she was talking about. Aunt Vi pursed her lips and nodded her head, but I didn't think she was listening properly.

'Very handsome man as well,' Aunt Doll added.

'Eden? Handsome? He's a right nancy boy, if you ask me.' No one had asked Nanny, but she said it anyway.

'Mum!'

Mum and the aunts nudged Nanny and eyeballed her in my

direction. Nanny looked straight at me. I pretended to choose a crayon, and they all pretended I hadn't heard anything. I knew Mum knew I had. Aunt Flo was sent to check on the joint in the oven.

'Don't touch it, just look at it,' My mum called out to her.

Aunt Doll 'umm'-ed with concern and decided to go and check the meat herself. Aunt Flo mustn't be seen to put a finger near it. 'You never know where those fingers of hers have been, scratching her head and all sorts,' I remembered someone once saying. They called her 'nitty Nora' behind her back and that was one of the reasons why I never got too close to her. My dad had told me that a flea could jump as high as Big Ben, but not to worry because they had no reason to leave Flo's head to get to mine. I never quite believed him. Pattie told me her mum didn't have nits, but I never quite believed her either.

Aunt Doll came back, with Aunt Flo following dozily behind. 'It looks almost the same as when you put it in, Mum. I hope your stove's not playing up. That'd be all we need today,' Aunt Doll warned.

She never mentioned my cousins playing in the cold passage. Maybe she preferred her Ron and Barbara staying out there and not listening to what I was hearing. The vegetables were peeled and chopped and they all gave themselves a fag break. Aunt Vi wrapped the peelings up in the newspaper and was just about to throw them into the fire when my mum got all upset.

'Don't, Vi. Not on the fire, for fuck's sake.'

'No, not on the fire, Vi. It's bad luck and ungodly,' Aunt Doll said patiently. 'And they're damp, they might put it out.'

Aunt Vi and Nanny laughed. Aunt Flo looked nervous and rolled and blinked her eyes in that funny way of hers.

'Ungodly? Well, I've heard it all now,' said Aunt Vi. She brought the parcel back to the table and left it there.

I looked at Pattie – I didn't quite know what for, perhaps some clue as to who was right or wrong about the peelings. She didn't look up, just stared straight ahead into the fire.

Something was happening at the table. The chairs had been pulled in closer and Nanny was speaking in her secretive whisper. I could tell my mum didn't want to be part of this conversation, because she examined Buster who was now asleep on her lap. Aunt Vi must have been armed with the facts already because she tried to warn Nanny to shut up. She did this by sitting back as far she could on her chair, so that Aunt Doll wouldn't catch her, and giving Nanny a big stare. But Nanny carried on until it finally dawned on Aunt Doll what she was saying. And Nanny realized she must have said a sentence too much.

'You've done what?' Aunt Doll was half standing up.

I could tell that Aunt Doll was fuming and that Aunt Vi already knew whatever it was that Nanny was saying. Aunt Flo was on edge and I could tell my mum was waiting for another 'performance'. We both knew Nanny was going to turn round in a minute, look at me as if she was dying, and hold out her arms for me to run into.

I was about to go to her when I saw my mum give me a look, so I stayed in the middle of the room, not knowing which way to turn. Then I went and cuddled Nanny and the steam went out of the room.

'I'm sorry, Doll, I had no choice. I'm trying to feed the five thousand here. Me and your dad haven't got two ha'pennies to rub together. I haven't even told him. I'll get us another one the minute I get myself straight.' Nanny sounded . . . I don't know, I felt sorry for her.

'What do they need life insurance for? When they drop dead we'll just leave them to medical research.' Aunt Vi was laughing.

'I'm sorry, Vi, but me and my Len don't have a pot to piss in either. I've been coming over here every fucking Friday, as well you know, like some fucking silly drawers, giving her half a crown a week for their life insurance. Four years I've been forking out for this.'

'Calm down, Doll. I have been paying it in. All but last month. I cashed it in then. Gospel. I needed it for Christmas.'

'You're not supposed to touch it, you silly old cow. I bet you didn't get anywhere near as much as I'd already paid in. By rights, that's my money, it's me you should be giving it back to.' Aunt Doll was giving in and giving up.

Nanny went on about how she had to look after Pattie along with everything else, and that Flo didn't have a job so she had to feed her as well. They all turned on Flo and said it was about time a lazy bastard like her found herself a job. Aunt Flo tried to say she'd been looking, but they wouldn't let her finish. She left the table in tears. I grabbed that moment to get back to the hearth. Pattie went and followed her mum into the scullery.

'If you're Betty Grable and your legs are your fortune then it might be worth having some sort of insurance policy, but quite frankly, once you're gone you're gone. Put me wherever you like, I'm not going to know anything about it, am I? What will I care?' Nanny said.

'What happened during the war when whole families were wiped out in one go? Who got the insurance money then?' Aunt Vi asked.

They mulled over that question for a while, laughed amongst themselves, and the impending storm was gone. Nanny told tales of the war and moving house all the time to save their lives. They took the piss out of her and said it wasn't to save *their* lives, it was to save herself from going to prison.

Prison. My nan in prison?

'If there's another war, we're not going to know anything about it, are we? The Yanks can't wait to drop another atom bomb and that will be the end of the lot of us.' Mum always said the word 'Yanks' as if they were the scum of the earth. In her opinion, the only things they were good for were acting in films, tap dancing, and making money.

I knew that when I grew up I must not marry a Yank.

CHAPTER FOUR

Mary

*T*he rat-tat-tatting of the First World War was over.

Six days after the Christmas of 1919, Mary popped out another daughter: Doris Clara, for ever after called Doll. Mary had been married nine months and this was the second birth Bob had missed. He was somewhere in the Indian Ocean. That's all she and Clara knew.

Nineteen-year-old Mary struggled with two babies the best she could. In the morning, come rain or shine, she would put Flo in her pram outside the front door and leave her there – for hours. Clara would sneak out on really bad days, bring the baby into the warm, and fret about what was happening upstairs. One bright March day, Flo, eighteen months old and too big for her pram, stood up, fell out, and broke her skull. Clara heard the pram tip over and was first on the scene. There was Flo, with her eyes and mouth wide open, silent. Blood haloing her head. She was as dead as a doornail. 'Mar-e-e-e-e-e-e!' Clara screamed. Neighbours flew out of their houses faster than Mary managed to get down the stairs. For the first few seconds, the women stared, frozen, at the broken doll on the pavement. Mary wobbled and had to be sat down on the wall. Clara dragged some of her senses into focus, picked the baby up, and heartbreakingly stretched her arms full out, displaying Flo to the gods. Flo started to gurgle and roll her eyes.

By the time Mrs Balkwell from next door had cycled to the

butcher's and made the phone call, it must have been twenty minutes before the ambulance arrived.

They didn't know where they were, which hospital they were in, or what was happening. Three-month-old Doll was bawling for her mother's milk, but Clara and Mary didn't seem to be able to hear her. Flo had been rushed away somewhere down the corridors of this huge place. They waited two hours in pasty-faced silence before a nurse came and told them to go home for now and come back again in the afternoon. They didn't ask if she would live or die; they didn't ask what was being done to her. They did as they were told and left.

Out in the daylight, Clara was shoved this way and that by the busy market crowd, while Mary tried to keep a hold on Doll, who was yelling and squirming for food and a clean bum. They worked out where they were: Whitechapel High Street, outside the London Hospital. It would take two trams and a bit of a walk to get them home to West Ham, and by the time they got there they would have no more than half an hour before turning round to come back to the hospital.

Doll got cleaned up and fed eventually, and Mrs Balkwell, who had been waiting on tenterhooks for news, made them strong sugary tea and bread with jam. She thought it was for the best if the baby stayed with her for the rest of the afternoon while Clara and Mary got back to poor little Flo.

Days walked into weeks. Flo, completely unaware, got visits on Wednesday afternoons from Mary and on Friday afternoons from Clara. In their hearts, they both prepared themselves for a funeral, although it was never talked about.

Six weeks later, Flo was brought home. Bald, a tin plate in her head, and a different look in her eye. Her epileptic fits frightened Mary; they reeked of the Devil. Baby Flo had to go – downstairs to Clara.

It was never mentioned to the two girls that they were sisters, and the subject never came up. Both of them called Mary 'Mum' and Clara 'Nanny', and that was good enough for everyone. Flo was better fed, better dressed, her clothes got washed *and* ironed, and her boots got polished. Doll would get the hand-me-downs. Flo would be for ever different.

When Uncle William was home from sea, Flo got toffees, sometimes Bible stories, and she was allowed to stroke the Chinaman off the top shelf. He was a beautiful oriental carving, with a full set of real ivory dentures. Uncle William would tell her about the sea, the countries he'd been to, the ships he'd seen sunk, and how he came by the Chinaman. It was all pointless in a way because, whatever Flo heard, it would float round her head, bounce off her tin plate, and disappear into the wallpaper.

William was a 'confirmed bachelor', whatever that might have meant in those days. He was six years older than Bob, adored his mother, collected exotic objects, and always had a pocketful of toffees to hand out. Clara would be the only woman in his life. He was probably a bit too much of a challenge for sauce-box Mary, so it's unlikely that she ever did a turn for him, however desperate she might have been for the money.

Bob loved his little Mary, loved his mother, loved the sea, and feared his God. He believed in God because he had to: God's church was the oceans, and the Devil was everywhere with his sirens and mermaids, sharks and pirates. When he was pissed he'd read the Bible aloud in the hope of jogging the Almighty's memory of Bob Roberts's saintliness.

For Mary, the Almighty was the bailiff that would never get paid. Her love was good linen and hard cash. She'd discovered tallymen – hire purchase for the poor, her gentleman callers. She knew all of them on the sly. Clara had a good idea what she was up to, but it was never mentioned. Mary would order the best linens, curtains, towels, and occasionally long-life underwear, then tout them round the streets and sell them for almost half the price the tallyman charged. Paying him back was for another day. Money was her lifelong passion: getting it, losing it, and getting it again.

The tallyman would come once a week for his payment. He rarely got it.

'Mummy says she's not in.'

'Nanny says she's not in.'

Her children, then her grandchildren, would all have to deliver this doorstep mantra at some point in their lives.

A court order. Oh, fuck. The promise of prison.

Mary knew that, at three and a half, Flo, happy as Larry living and sleeping with Clara, probably wouldn't even notice that anything was different. But Doll was only eighteen months old, what would become of her?

Mary would often stare at the Chinaman and he would stare back. She knew he was worth a lot of money, and she knew the Chinaman knew that she knew it. Ivory teeth. They were better than her own.

'Where's the Chinaman, Flo?' Mary knew exactly where he was.

'High on a shelf where he can talk to God in private,' whispered Flo.

The men were back at sea. The baby was asleep. Clara had just shouted up that she was going to the herbalist and would she keep an eye on Florence? Mary had about ten minutes with Flo and the front doorstep all to herself.

'Well, he's finished with God now, cos God's talking to me. And God wants me to have a few quiet words with the Chinaman.'

'I can't hear anything,' stuttered Flo, feeling a bit on edge and holding on to her crotch.

'God's not got all day and neither have I. Go and get him, you

dozy mare. Climb on one of the dining chairs if you can't reach.'
Mary pushed her queer daughter into the house; she needed to
stay on the lookout for the returning Clara, and she had to move
fast. The toddler didn't understand what was expected of her
and whimpered away the precious time. Mary would have to
take a chance. She dashed down the hallway to Clara's back
room; the Chinaman, centre-stage on the shelf by the fireplace,
was snatched and rushed to the front step. It was eleven o'clock
in the morning, a Wednesday, and hardly anybody was about.
The bone-cracking February weather had kept all the other
housewives indoors, away from each other and their over-the-
wall gossip. Mother and daughter shivered in the bright winter
sunshine, from cold and from nerves.

Flo did as she was told and held on to the head while the other
eight or so inches of the carved torso were wedged between
Mary's legs so that Mary could keep a firm grip while she tried
to push her fat little fingers into the tiny slit of a mouth. She
couldn't do it, she couldn't get a purchase anywhere to fiddle
them out: the ivory teeth wouldn't budge. Mary tried punching
them out and hoped they wouldn't fall through into the inside
of the head and be lost for ever. When Flo saw her mother's cut
and bleeding fist she started to snivel with worry.

Searching upstairs for pliers, a fork, anything, Mary heard the
defeat: she was too late, Clara was back. She could hear Flo
mumbling on a single long breath: 'I can't say anything because
it's private and God can't talk Chinese anyway so what's the
point and he bit Mum when she punched him and she could go
to prison for that but I think *he* should go to prison.'

Mary sauntered down the stairs to the front door with a
potato and peeler in one hand and the sleeping Doll slung
over her shoulder, a picture of innocence. After a lot of toing
and froing and whys and hows, Flo, of course, got the blame.
She must have been having one of her turns.

The Chinaman, which Clara held like a precious baby in her arms, grinned across the threshold at Mary and she thought she saw the pink wet flicker of a tongue glisten through his wealthy mouth.

No ivory teeth meant no money, and Mary went to Holloway prison. She was twenty-two years old. Clara couldn't or wouldn't help her – help pay off the tallyman to stop all this. She didn't go to the court to defend her daughter-in-law or to hear the charges. The best that Clara could offer was to look after the girls. Doll moved downstairs with Flo. If anyone asked, Mary was in 'hospital'.

Three months away, where Mary had extra time to hone her performance skills. There she learned that cockiness and lip would get you into more trouble than they were worth. She could read and write, which came in dead handy behind bars. The other prisoners gave her two smokes per letter. To be indispensable was survival, and before long everyone needed something from Mary. She could fight her way out of trouble if she had to, but preferred the spider's web of brain-befuddling lingo. The girls allowed themselves to fall for her gift of the gab, and Mary would wheedle her way under their skins.

Bob and William were away at sea and weren't expected home for another two months. We'll never know what Mary told Bob about how and why she was in prison, but it won't have been the truth. When he did find out where she was, she was safe from a good hiding, out of reach behind bars. The fire had gone out of him by the time of her release, and prison was never mentioned again.

The Chinaman's presence would continue to torture Mary. He took the piss out of her every time she looked at him. She would never get the better of the Chinaman. He haunted her. Some nights he would come and float above her bed. In the dark Mary would punch and kick, effing and blinding like a banshee, and bashing little Doll who slept beside her. Doll never saw the phantom, but by the age of four she realized that it was a good move to say she did, so she could get her mother back to bed.

'It's gone now, Mum.'

'I'll fucking have him, slitty-eyed little bastard.'

Thursday nights were always bad: the tallyman came on a Friday.

Vi was the first of the babies to arrive while Bob was at home – another bloody girl. It was 1923.

Mary was used to life without Bob and in many ways preferred it. He was usually away for nine months and home for three. Those three months could seem endless for both of them. Bob and William always started their leave with excitement. Excitement at seeing their mother, seeing the kids, eating women's food, not sailors' food, telling their stories, going to the pub. After three weeks, they were bored and out of place, and Mary had to keep on her toes to stop Bob from discovering her chicanery. Every Friday morning at nine o'clock she would leave the house and say she was meeting her mother 'up the top'. 'Up the top' was the main road, where there was no mother to meet; the only person she was meeting was the tallyman, before he got to her door.

Upstairs, Mary would roll a fag and plot how to get tomorrow's dinner. If she baked Bob one of her rice puddings with a nutmeg crust, she could nearly always get some extra money out of him, so long as she delivered before he went to the pub. If she wanted extra extra, she would unplait her hair, give it a good brush, and let it hang like Delilah's promise down her back.

She fell pregnant every time he was home, but her body was tired. Senna-pod tea didn't just evacuate the bowels, on a good day it could purge the body of all sorts of unwanted luggage.

Winifred was born on 9 March 1927. Four daughters. Flo was nine, Doll was eight and Vi was four. Mary had the beginnings of her servants.

The minute Bob's money order arrived, she would pay off the debts she had to, buy more stuff off the tallyman and start selling again. Her wedding ring lived in the pawnshop, to be redeemed before Bob got home from sea. Married life and motherhood were her unredeemed pledge.

When 'Mummy says she's not in' didn't work, and the tallyman wouldn't go away without payment, she'd keep him quiet with sex and the promise afterwards that she'd tell his wife if he didn't behave himself. He wasn't going to say anything, was he? If he did, he'd lose his job, his wife, and Bob Roberts would knock his fucking teeth out.

Eighteen months after the birth of Win, baby Robert was born, and he was the spit of Bob, thank the Lord. No doubt about it, with his black hair and square nose. The tallyman was ginger, with a pencil for a nose. Bob was over the moon – a son at last. This boy would go places, be somebody, and look after them in their old age. His girls would go places as well, beyond anything he could have imagined.

With young Flo skimming the surface of dreamland downstairs, Doll and Vi looked after the two babies upstairs, helped with the housework, ran errands, and sometimes played the leading roles in 'Finding a Pot to Piss In'. Vi hated it and Doll got on with it. Vi would always hate it and Doll would always get on with it.

Brutal weather would aid and abet her brutal tactics and only the hardest heart could turn Mary and her soaking-wet girls away. The pram, with Win and Robert squashed in and filled to the brim with curtains and sheets, would be dragged over the stranger's front step and into the warmth. Over a cup of tea, act two would begin: 'When's he get paid? Don't worry, darling, give it to me on Thursday ... No, that's all right, I'll come and get it, or one of me girls. Pure Irish linen they are, same as they use on the Cunard line, can't buy them from a shop y'know.' Doll or Vi would trudge round to collect the money a week later, rain or shine.

By the time Vi was about seven, she couldn't be trusted to do it. When *she* went, she'd be on the missing list for hours and come back empty-handed, having 'lost' the money or 'found nobody in'. If Flo was slow and dreamy and as readable as a book in large print, and Doll was straightforward and energetic and kind, then Vi was shifty, a natural fibber. When Vi wasn't believed, she'd get a good hiding; when she *was* believed, Mary would tear round to whoever owed her and *they'd* get a good hiding. Poor Mrs Thingy would lose a couple of teeth and clumps of hair, get two black eyes, and the police would be called. All over a desperately needed half-crown. When the National Health gave her the free gift of vicious-looking dentures, Mary would give a five-second warning before she started fighting. She'd take her teeth out, throw them in a corner, and everyone would duck.

Mary would stand in the dock many, many times, but she never again went to prison. Somehow, every magistrate she ever came up against was charmed by the harshness of her existence. Her tiny frame, lovely red hair, and green eyes brimming with nervous tears could splinter the hardest of hearts. Especially when compared to the shabby-suited tallyman with his greedy briefcase full of unpaid debts.

Mary was now thirty-one with five kids and herself to feed, but Bob always came back from sea with something.

'I hope you're taking that back with you when you go. I can't feed myself, let alone that.'

'Mary, Mary, Mary, it only needs scraps.'

'Scraps? We live on scraps. What scrap of a scrap are you thinking of?'

The monkey savaged the kids, savaged Mary, and created mayhem.

Bob and his monkey were more popular down the pub than indoors. They became a bit of a turn. Bob played his squeezebox and the customers would treat him to a few free pints, and the monkey would get some peanuts and the odd sip of gin. They'd stay until closing time and then roll home well pissed. Once indoors, Bob would take off the monkey's collar and lead and enjoy watching it chase Mary round the flat. She worked out that she might as well go down the pub with them, rather than sit and dread their homecoming, especially if there was a chance of a free half-pint.

After a night out, quiet gentle Bob would forget about his adoration of little Mary Burke, would forget that he was upsetting his mother and brother downstairs, and would only remember the festering poverty of his life. His unpredictable violence would be allowed to go so far, then, when she'd just about had enough, Mary would turn into Irish rain, drenching all around her in maudlin sentiment, and flop into bed, breaking everyone's heart. Next morning, the roles would be reversed. As he tried to get his soul back together, Bob would be sent down to apologize to his mother, with Mary earwigging at the top of the stairs.

Mary was hanging out of her upstairs window, winding in the pulley, pretending to collect her clean washing. In the yard below, directly underneath her, was a rainwater butt.

Plop.

She ran downstairs and through Clara's scullery, screaming, 'I've dropped me pegs.'

Holding the canvas bag under the water, little streaks of blood mingled with the dead flies and old leaves floating on the top. He had managed to bite Mary one last time before she had knocked him unconscious with the flat iron. She dragged him out, wrung him out, rolled him into her apron, and took him inside. Then she went on her walkabout with the infants. Three miles away from her own front door, between Forest Gate and Stratford Broadway, the monkey was dropped into somebody's coal-hole.

Bob went back to sea, miserable. Over the years he would ask her what had really happened, and over the years she would tell him what hadn't really happened, depending on her mood and his:

'We ate him, with onions, and so did you, remember?'

Or:

'Chased old Mrs Balkwell's cat; never seen again, either of them.'

Or:

'Fell on the line at Plaistow station. Suicide, the coroner said.'

Boxing Day 1956

The basement had almost warmed up, with still freezing cold bits here and there. My aunts piled their coats into my arms. Aunt Doll's posh coat had been carefully folded and laid on top of Pattie's, Nanny's, Mum's, and mine and I went and put them next door on Nanny and Granddad's bed. Aunt Flo could do her own. The bedroom was particularly freezing.

The roasting lamb was steaming up the scullery and the smell of it cosied our noses and throats. Nanny's oven always steamed up the scullery because the door didn't fit properly. She could still cook really delicious meat, though, and everyone fought for her roast potatoes. Whenever her potatoes were praised she'd give one of her looks, as if everyone were feeble-minded, and say: 'King Edwards. That's all it is. You can never go wrong with a King Edward. You don't want to buy any of these artsy-fartsy waxy ones, they're fucking useless.'

'Any of these artsy-fartsy waxy ones, they're fucking useless,' we all joined in together.

The 'fucking useless' had slipped out of my mouth before I knew it. All of them spun their faces towards me. They laughed very loudly and let it go. The laughter didn't last long.

My cousins came in from the passage. They were frozen stiff now and Aunt Vi's George (always called Little George owing to the fact that we already had a Big George) pushed everyone out of the way to get warmed first.

Gangly Little George, in long trousers now that he had started at secondary modern school, had skin the colour of strong tea and frizzy hair like a permed coconut. His grey trousers, short grey school blazer, and flannel shirt gave him a slightly grubby look. Little George's brother Gary was very black. That wasn't the only reason he was called 'Black Gary'. We had another Gary, a white baby Gary, upstairs, almost the same age as our Buster. We could have called them Little Gary and Big Gary, I suppose, but 'Black' seemed easier. He was still a short trousers and long socks little boy. The flat greyness of his clothes couldn't quieten the polish of his skin and his shiny hair. They weren't my favourite cousins. I was a bit nervous of Little George and his bony elbows. He moved too fast and I felt he might do something dangerous any minute, just like Aunt Vi. Black Gary cried and whined all the time, so he was no fun at all, just like Aunt Flo.

Pattie was my favourite; I pretended she was my big sister. She had lovely white skin, a thin long nose, and hair like my mum's. Her gums were bigger than her teeth, though, and when her mouth was shut it looked as if she had been punched in the face. Mostly she let her mouth have its way and stay hanging open. If it hadn't been for the gums, I would have wanted to look like her, but I didn't want to be her. Nanny liked me best.

Barbara was six and she never got her frock or white ankle-socks dirty. I was fed up with hearing how beautiful she was, and how many hearts she was going to break when she grew up. Anyone would look lovely in a royal blue coat with black velvet collar. I was going to have a coat like that one day, but I would choose green, not a poncey blue. Her dark eyebrows were too close together and she had hairy arms. My mum said she was spoilt. Barbara always peered at the rest of us as if we smelt. Her big brother, Ron, was my next favourite cousin – except he wasn't big. Even though he was eleven, he was the same size as me. He didn't have to wear his school clothes like Little George and Black Gary. He had a boy's version of Barbara's coat over brown corduroy short trousers and a matching jacket. He said that at his grammar school the boys weren't allowed long trousers until they were thirteen. Little George, who definitely wasn't clever enough for grammar school, didn't believe him and called him a poof. Ron was the only blond in the family, so that must have been what Little George was referring to. Aunt Vi's yellow hair didn't count – she'd got it from the chemist's.

My cousins were suddenly ordered to play out in the backyard, except for Pattie who was allowed to remain indoors so that she could keep brewing tea and stoking the fire. I was allowed to stay to keep Buster occupied.

The atmosphere was still simmering and my mum and the aunts kept giving each other deep looks, as if their words were jumping silently from their mouths into their eyeballs. Aunt Flo was the only one watching Nanny. Nanny looked at the alarm clock on the mantelshelf and went out of the door, muttering something about checking the dinner. Silence. It was best to be invisible and wait for someone to start speaking. I'd seen the black eye myself, so I knew something bad had occurred.

It was only ten minutes ago that Aunt Carol had come down to say that there had been a change of plan and that now she was going round to Tony's mother's for their dinner. Her two babies, stuffed into one big pram, were already outside in the street with the Galoot, the family name for Tony. He had snuck out of the upstairs front door, bouncing the pram down the steps.

Messing up the dinner business was nowhere near as bad as the sight of eighteen-year-old Carol. Her lovely face was red and puffy, and one eye was now a different shape from the other, with purple and pink lines coming from her nose to her cheekbone. Baby Gary had accidentally headbutted her when she'd lifted him up from his po, she'd told them.

'Is that the same story you're going to tell his mother?' Nanny demanded.

That was what made Aunt Doll tell us kids to get out into the backyard, but in the noisy skedaddle I crept under the dining table with Buster. Pattie made herself scarce getting more coal from the coal-hole. My mum was really angry and got straight to the point:

'Has he given you a right-hander?'

Then they all started. Aunt Vi asked, 'Why's he airing his heels outside there? Trying to get away before the others get back from the pub? Got something to be ashamed of, has he?'

'Carol, if he's walloped you, we're going to have to nip this in the bud right now. We're not having any of this.' Aunt Doll had a gentle quiver in her voice.

'And the baby's head is perfectly all right, is it?' Nanny sneered.

'Will you leave off and stop going on the rampage over nothing. Just because you don't like him. I'll say it again. I hit my fucking head on the baby's head, all right?' Carol shouted, and with that she flounced out of the door and was gone.

The front door rat-tatted immediately. She had shut Pattie out in the cold. That's when I crawled out from under the table to let her back in and saw Aunt Flo looking at Nanny, and Nanny looking at the clock and then leaving to go and see to the meat.

I got back as quickly as possible so as to be around the fire and breathe in the grown-ups' bubbling blood. The silence was dense with zipped-up words, and I started to feel in the way and a bit nosy. I made myself look busy and got Buster from under the table where he was pulling tufts and ropy bits out of the balding carpet and brought him near the fire with me and Pattie, who was soundlessly plaiting old newspapers ready to become tomorrow's kindling.

I took a big page and showed Buster how to make pointy

party hats. It was funny watching him try and fold a straight line when all he could manage was tearing or scrunching it into shreds. It kept him quiet for ages.

'Shut your mouth, Flo, you look like a postcard of Cheddar Gorge,' Aunt Vi snapped. For a second her voice had fired into the room like a bullet. Then it all went very quiet again.

Aunt Flo put her lips together, slowly took the hairgrip out of her hair, looked at it, and put it back exactly where it had been before. Then she picked a brown speckled feather off her cardigan and holding it up, wondered what she should do with it. Everyone was staring at her, even me. Aunt Doll took the feather and threw it away. Aunt Flo stared at something private in her head, made a squeaky sound, stood up, holding her crotch, and Lettuce-Leafed out of the room. Aunt Doll looked sad, Aunt Vi lit up a fag, and Mum kissed the top of Lionel's head.

Baby Lionel was fast asleep on Mum's lap, and I could tell that the weight of him had made her arm go dead because she was looking round for somewhere safe to lay him.

'Give him here,' Aunt Doll whispered, and Lionel was handed over.

Nanny came back in, mumbling that Flo had pissed herself and was upstairs changing her drawers. She said it in a tone that meant, 'That's all I need on top of everything else.' How long would it be before someone broke the silence? Who would go first? I plonked the paper hat on Buster's head and knew it would have to be Aunt Vi.

'What are you going to do, Mum, when he murders her? It won't stop at a black eye, believe you me. Once a bloke starts that malarkey it will only go from bad to worse.' Aunt Vi sounded very important. They started to whisper and I couldn't catch it all, but I knew they were very serious. I caught snippets of 'If my Bill laid a finger on me that would be it,' and 'For

Christ's sake, let's leave it alone now and see how it goes.' Nanny suggested to my mum that my new dad should have a word with the Galoot, but Mum said that would be a waste of time because he wouldn't get himself involved in any of this. By the time they had gone round the houses looking at the problem this way and that – who to tell, who not to tell – it ended up sounding not so very important any more. It was as if they had licked the 'Carol problem' away with their tongues.

The cousins screamed down the passage and back into the warm, overexcited, and starving hungry. Bony Little George pushed everyone out of the way so as to get as close to the fire as he could without actually walking on the coals. Ron and Barbara had grubby faces and hands and were giggling as they pretended to wipe off the dirt onto each other's clothes. Black Gary sidled his way onto one side of the hearth to get a warm-up.

Aunt Vi took charge. 'Right you lot, out in that scullery, wash your faces and hands and get upstairs to Carol and Tony's. Play up there, go on, there's a nice electric fire you can sit round. Go on, off you go.'

Pattie didn't know which way to turn. Was she supposed to follow them or stay put? She stayed put, waiting for further orders. I knew that if I followed them upstairs I would have to take Buster with me and I wouldn't be able to play properly. I took a chance and decided to stay where I was. The noise of their charging about woke Lionel up; he started bawling and kicking his legs, so Aunt Doll handed him back to Mum. Lionel's crying gave Buster the idea of joining in. He threw his newspaper hat onto the fire, screamed a war dance at the flames, and ran around trying to find things to burn. I asked Nanny if I could go into the scullery and make some bread and dripping to keep him quiet.

I was sitting on the floor with my back to the sideboard and my face frizzing with the heat from the fire. Buster had slurped his bread into wet little strings until he had fallen asleep in my lap. His head was so heavy that it pinned me into an immovable position. I stared into the hobs of hell and listened. They talked of murder.

'Don't you let the old man know I'm telling you all this. He won't have it mentioned. His mother was very ashamed of it. I don't know why, the silly old cow. I mean, she didn't do it, did she?' Nanny said this in an offhand voice.

'Where were we when all this was going on?' asked Aunt Vi.

'Well, as luck would have it, the King was abdicating at the time, so the papers were full of that. I mean, it was in all the papers, but Mrs Simpson was taking the brunt of it, wasn't she? Anyway, poor old Ernest died in Brixton prison hospital on the very day he was to stand trial. Well, it wasn't a trial really, because he'd admitted it the month before when it all happened, just a formality for sentencing. He would have hung, I reckon. If he had managed to get to court proper, he would have bumped into Bette Davis who was in the same court suing Warner Brothers for overwork or something.'

Nanny had said, 'He would have hung, I reckon.' Who? How can you die before you're hung? Do they hang dead bodies? They rattled on about Mrs Simpson and Bette Davis. I thought they were never going to get back to this Ernest.

'Well, who was he? Do we have any of his blood? What's he to do with us?' Aunt Vi snapped.

'Do you think that meat's all right, Mum? Must be nearly time to put the spuds on,' my mum said.

Lionel had quietened down now that he had her teat in his mouth. Nanny looked at the clock again and said that no, they had another half-hour before it was all systems go with the veg.

I looked at Pattie, who was making dancing ladies out of

torn-up newspaper. Was she thinking about blood-sharing and meat-roasting? Did dead hanging bodies smell like the lamb burning in the scullery? I thought of dinner and how I was going to eyeball Mum so that I got only roasties and no meat.

Meat with string for a hanging.

'So he's not the Burke side of the family?' Aunt Doll sounded surprised.

'Trust you to think that. No, he's fucking not. Clara Roberts with all her airs and graces had a few dark horses as well, y'know.'

Nanny was offended, and I couldn't work out why.

Aunt Flo slipped back into the room with her clean drawers on and sat back in her place. Pattie looked up at her, but Flo was pondering whether to pinch one of Aunt Vi's fags. Everyone read her intentions – even me – and at the same moment all hands pushed the packet of Player's Weights towards her. She mumbled a 'ta' and lit up.

'When you say "murder", do you really mean murder, or are you making too much of it?' Aunt Doll asked.

'Too much of it? Do us a favour. He was knocking off his landlady, who must've been a right old tom, if you ask me. She was – what? sixty-one or something? I mean, Ernest was only my age now, fifty-six. Anyway, whatever was going on, she brings him his clean underwear while he's having a bath. Now, if you're not knocking each other off, why else would you swan into a naked man in the bath, as bold as brass? Before she knows what's hit her, he's dragged her into the water, she bangs her head on the side, and he holds her down till she's done for.'

'But who was he to Dad?' Aunt Doll asked.

'Sounds choice, don't it?' Mum said.

'He was your Granny Roberts's brother, which makes him Dad's uncle and your great-uncle. And no, we never clapped eyes on him, as far as I know.'

'How did he die? He top himself or something?' Aunt Vi sounded nosy, but not that interested.

My mum was always trying to put me straight about Nanny. She said she was a bit of a Tom Pepper and you couldn't trust anything she said, and that I must never 'fall into her clutches' if I knew what was best for me. Well, if Nanny was such a fibber, why were we all ears listening to her now? I could tell that Mum was not best pleased with all this talk of murder. Probably because Nanny was having little digs about someone my mum liked, being a bit snipe-nosed about this other Granny Roberts, who had died before I was born.

I couldn't wait for the story to go on.

Please, Buster, don't wake up. Don't move.

'I don't know why we're all dancing round this. We knew years ago that something had gone on. Don't you remember when I came back from that spiritualist? He told me something then, just after my Rob was born, and when I asked you and Dad about it you both went mad.' Mum reminded them.

They talked about her visit to the spiritualist and how it had frightened Mum so much that she had woken up in the middle of the night screaming, with her hair 'literally' standing on end.

'It was. It was standing straight up in the air, as if she'd been electrocuted. Silly cow, the noise of the trains rumbling past was what she could hear, not anything else. Ghosts? Do us a favour!' Nanny said.

Aunt Doll brought up the Chinaman and how Nanny used to be frightened of him. 'She'd kick and holler and punch her fists all night. It was murder. I was only a toddler; sometimes I'd get a right-hander by mistake. Terrible nightmares she'd have. He was coming to cut her throat, according to her. So you used to believe in ghosts one time, Mother, didn't you?' Aunt Doll had got the others going now.

'Yeah, yeah, take the piss . . .' Nanny was letting it go.

'Don't laugh, Doll, I was there when he bit her, I was only little,' Aunt Flo whispered.

They made each other laugh remembering some long-ago time, and when they were like this together something safe was in the air. It was one voice with different curves, one language I didn't know but understood. *Billy Cotton's Bandshow* with extra trumpets.

'Do you know, as far as I'm aware, Clara Roberts never went to see her brother once?' Nanny pulled the strings and got their full attention once more.

I wanted to turn round and see what was going on, but my whole body and legs had gone dead with the weight of Buster sleeping and dribbling on me. Pattie, in a trance, scrutinized the fire. Asleep with her eyes open.

Nanny was ready for her close-up.

'Ernest Bauckham. That was his name. B-A-U-C-K-H-A-M. Funny spelling, isn't it? A touch of the Kraut in the family. Anyway, once he's done her in, he arrives a few hours later in Whitechapel and goes to Leman Street police station to give himself up. How he got the seven or eight miles from Forest Gate, we'll never know. I think he stopped at a few pubs on the way. I know more about it than your dad, or anyone, if truth be told, because I'd sneak out and read the papers down the shop. Old Clara wouldn't have any papers in the house while it was all going on. I had to laugh, though. Listen to this. Apparently, once the police had gone to the house and seen the poor old cow floating in his dirty bath water, they came back to see him in Leman Street station to take a full statement. They told him what they'd found.'

'"She's dead, then?" That's what he said to them, "She's dead then?" He'd already fucking told them that he'd held her down and stayed there for about an hour till the water got cold. What was he thinking? That she'd fallen in with a snorkel?'

'He wasn't a real murderer, then, was he, not if he gave himself up?' Aunt Vi said. 'Hardly makes him Dr Crippen.'

'What did the neighbours make of it?' asked Aunt Doll.

'They didn't. They had no idea he was Clara's brother, and she wasn't going to let on, was she? People did mention it, but, as I say, they were more interested in the King. It all happened in four weeks. He knew he was dying with throat cancer or something. That's why he gave himself up, I reckon. Bonk. Four weeks later he's gone. The papers said that he killed her because he loved her and he'd seen her in the pub larking about with another bloke. Now, if that's not some old tom, I don't know what is. He's buried in unconsecrated ground, you know. In Brixton nick, I think. That's the big disgrace – well, it was then, I'm not sure if people care so much about that sort of thing now. Give us a fag, Vi.'

I felt something warm on my lap, coming from Buster's nappy.

'Mum. Mum. He's done a cacar.' I looked to her for help, but her arms were already full with the baby. Aunt Doll came for Buster and made a face about the smell. I laughed.

'I was nearly murdered once,' piped up Aunt Flo.

'What went wrong?' Nanny asked her.

CHAPTER FIVE

Mary

*I*t was 1936 and the ocean had spewed Bob back onto dry land for ever. After months of being out of work, along with almost everyone else he knew, he managed to lie his way into becoming an engineer for Lyons Corner Houses, maintaining their refrigeration units. Bob figured that as he knew how to make a wireless out of bits and pieces he could quickly learn how these newfangled things worked. Lyons Corner Houses had coffee and cake shops stretching from the City of London through to the West End. Office workers and idle ladies would lunch and gossip while being waited on by 'nippies'. These were smartly turned-out waitresses in black frocks with white caps and aprons. Being a nippy meant being nippy. Brother William found work as a railway porter, after a struggle. Mary was also on the lookout for a move.

Her debts with the tallymen were bigger than ever and she needed to disappear. Too many months with only Doll's wages to keep them all going had pushed her connivances to the limit. At fourteen, Doll had got a job through big sister Flo at the Aerated Bread Company in Stratford. She could walk there in half an hour. Flo and Doll were kitchen hands, hoping to get promotion to waitresses, where there was always the chance of the odd tip. After two years of this hot, sweaty skivvying, Doll had had enough and her pretend day 'off sick' had paid off. She had passed the exam to become a nippy, ditched Aerated Bread and the long daily walk to work, and loved every minute of the third-class Tube ride to Marble Arch, up West, into posh-land. Once she'd settled in and made herself popular and reliable, she got Flo an interview. Somehow, with a little bit of training from Doll, Flo passed the test and was sent to the same Corner House. Being nippy would never be one of her gifts, and after two weeks of trying to get her to speed up the manageress surrendered and put Flo in the kitchen out of sight. Mary never had a sniff of Flo's wages: they were handed over to Clara for safe keeping. But two pay packets coming in were better than one, or none; and Vi, at thirteen, was only a year away from getting put to work.

Now that Bob was home for good, the two rooms upstairs were stifling Mary. One double bed and two single camp beds crowded the bedroom that Robert, Win, Vi, and Doll had to share. Doll and Win always slept together. Mary and Bob had their bed in the front room, which doubled as a seating area during the day, and when they were all at home it was unbearable. Win would go with Robert downstairs to Clara to keep out of their mum's way and the inevitable wallops. Downstairs and the inevitable goodies – a spoonful of delicious tinned evaporated milk, a toffee each, and, if their luck was in, an errand to run and a penny for their trouble.

Mary decided that if she moved away from the mother-in-law, she would be able to cajole Flo into moving with her and that would mean another pay packet to gamble with. This hungry thought made her more reckless with her buying and selling. She found a newly built house for rent in Becontree Heath for seventeen shillings and sixpence a week. Mary had never paid rent in her life and that was the sum total of Doll's earnings. Becontree Heath – almost Essex, almost countryside, miles from anywhere. The kids couldn't understand why they had to go so far away from their Granny and Uncle William. Everyone said another war was coming.

But Flo wasn't budging.

Mary gave Bob and Doll the new address, scribbled on two scraps of white butcher's paper. They would leave one house on their way to work and have to find the new one on the way home. Doll said she'd meet her dad at Liverpool Street station and they'd fathom the new geography out together. They were both leaving the only home that either of them had ever had.

Tearful 'Ta-ta's to Granny Roberts and Uncle William from the kids. No, Flo wasn't going to change her mind and yes, she was sure it was all going to be lovely in the countryside, but the tin plate in her head told her to stay where she was. One pay packet less.

Somehow Mary had charmed the coalman and his lorry into doing the move. Open to the elements, he had kindly laid down fresh sacks on the floor of the wagon, for them to pile the beds, table, sideboard, some kitchen chairs, and two cardboardy suitcases full of their lives on top. Win, Robert, and Vi then squeezed themselves on top of all that. Mary, of course, sat inside with the coalman. It rained.

Bob and Doll found their home eventually and arrived to damp beds, black-as-Newgate-knockers kids, and no dinner. He went to find a pub and slurped thoughts of having a guard dog.

They slept on the floor while the mattresses dried out, and stayed in their travelling clothes, covered in coal dust, until Mary got herself shipshape. Win and Robert went to their new school, but Vi couldn't be bothered to go, as she only had a few months left. Truth was, Mary hated being in the house alone: it was too quiet, too green, too much nature. Vi knew the truth and played on it.

There were five of these new houses, with fields at the back and a dirt track out the front. The dirt track was a ten-minute walk to the main road and some semblance of civilization. The other houses were still unoccupied. Sometimes cows would block their way and Bob's new dog would cause more mayhem than Win squirming with fear or Vi shouting abuse at the farmer. Mary hardly left the house. There was no street lighting, so when night-time came it fell like blindness. It was the biggest house the family had ever been in. Four large bedrooms upstairs off the turn-around landing and a lovely bathroom and inside lavatory. The bathroom had huge black and white tiles, and shiny black glass covering the side of the bath. A small window overlooked the path at the side of the house. Downstairs, to the right of the wide hall, was the front room with its beige tiled fireplace. It was a new style fireplace, called a 'fire surround'. The next room – with a window onto the muddy, churned-up back garden – was the dining room. Beyond that was a kitchen-scullery with butler-sink and draining boards on both sides, a brand new stove, shelves on the walls, and a built-in unit with two drawers above roomy cupboards. Blue and cream was the overall theme, apart from the red terracotta tiled floor.

The windows were a shape that Mary had never had to dress before and all her curtains were too long and skinny. These new 1930s' windows were much lower because the ceilings were lower, but they were wide – very wide. Every window would need new curtains, even though there was hardly anybody about to peer in.

The house had an immersion heater. Mary was frightened of this newfangled thing, for she'd never dealt with one before. If you waited an hour and didn't mind the cost, you could enjoy a good scrub in a room all to yourself. No more dragging in the zinc bath from the backyard, carrying the water – worse still, getting the water emptied when the job was done. No more freezing your balls off standing at the sink while you washed underneath your arches. Usually, though, Mary boiled the kettle. The bathroom got used on rainy days as a place to dry the washing.

Mary almost had enough beds, she had a sideboard, a table, and six wooden chairs. Her old double bed went upstairs in the front for her and Bob. Should the sideboard go in here or down in the front room? The other double bed was for Doll to have a room of her own; the two singles were for Win and young Robert. They wanted to share their room – they didn't fancy sleeping in the blackest of nights on their own. Vi was the one who needed a bed for her room; she couldn't wait for the privacy. For two weeks she slept on the floor until Mary finally took delivery of a camp bed, along with new curtains and sheets. She'd found a new tallyman to do business with. Even so, her few sticks of furniture couldn't stop this house looking bare-boned and unlived-in. For a start, there was nowhere to sit in the front room, and that was where the fire was.

1 Crowden Villas,
Becontree Heath,
Essex.
24 February 1936

Dear Mum and William,

Well, we're in. It's been a bit of a struggle to say the least, but the kids have got more room to run around in and we are not under each other's feet all the time. I'm sure you're more than pleased to have your house back to yourselves after all these years and not having to put up with us lot. We have not been able to use the front room yet as we haven't got anywhere to perch, which is a bit of a bind as it's the room with the fireplace in. We are all all right though, because we keep warm in the back room next to the scullery and I keep the stove on when everyone's home. I don't bother when it's just me because we can't afford it, so I keep my coat on and toil around the house. There's nothing else to do. It's so quiet here, I can go days without seeing another soul. The few shops that are here are half an hour's walk away, but I manage. I did see two respectable-looking old armchairs for sale in the rag-and-bone man's yard but down here everything is so dear. I think I'll have to wait till I get up to see you both and try and find something cheaper in Stratford.

Anyway, hope it's not too long before we clap eyes on each other. The kids send love, as do me and Bob.

Mary.

It worked. One Sunday morning they heard the sound of a lorry struggling through the muddy lane, and it stopped outside their house. There was Uncle William and the coalman unloading two carpets, two yellowy-gold armchairs with high backs, and a white-painted Lloyd Loom wicker chair with a padded seat in brown velvet.

Win put the kettle on, Mary cried, and Bob looked embarrassed.

'Don't worry about it – my pleasure. And they didn't cost that much,' William told them.

The coalman threw in a free sack of coal for such a nice cup of tea.

'Where did you get that?'

'He'll keep you company, out here in the wilds of nowhere, be a guard dog for you,' said Bob.

Mary stared at the black mongrel. It stared back and growled.

'He's called Blackie,' said Bob.

'Of course he fucking is.' She walked out into the scullery and stirred the stew.

When Mary moved she made sure her debts didn't follow her. It should have been a fresh start – money coming in, kids growing up – but somehow she was still struggling. Moving was expensive, what with the new linen and the curtains. She had new tallymen to hypnotize. Pretty windows – bread and scrape – but honest-looking windows.

Bob gave her two thirds of his wages; his third was for beer money and anything he might need to buy for his wirelesses. He found some kind of peace, an ocean-like aloneness, with his dog and his radios. He loved to fiddle about and mend old crystal radios, and sometimes when he had all the right bits he could make a brand new one. And he loved Blackie. Making radios was supposed to be a way of making some extra money, but somehow he ended up keeping most of them.

Doll, Robert, and Win loved Blackie as well. Mary and Vi ignored him or kicked him out of the way. He'd be let out first thing in the morning by Mary, before anyone else was up, to roam about and fend for himself. The shops were always his first port of call. He had a proper dog's life – pinching bones from the butcher, crusts from the baker, having lots of street-sex, finding other dogs to play with or fight with – and he learnt to tell the time. He'd wait outside the school and walk Robert and Win home, then dash off to have another adventure. At the end of his day, he would wait at the corner for Bob to come home, at the end of *his* day.

'Do all mums have a special mum's plate, Mum?' Win was dreaming up all sorts of visions as she pondered her mother's white plate with 'J. Lyons' printed on it. No one else was allowed to use this plate. This was Mary's plate

'No, Win, only this mum,' said Mary, dishing up the suet pudding. Blackie wedged himself between Win and Bob, staring lovingly up at them. Hunger made their teeth sweat; hunger made them size up who got the fattest portion.

Bob was reading the paper while he ate. Mary stared at the dog, slowly masticating the inside of her head, aggravating a thought to come out whole, and willing it to be worth a bob or two.

'Mum, if you broke the special mum's plate, would you have to buy another one?' Win had finished swallowing.

Robert had also finished, and was trying to read the backside of his dad's newspaper. Blackie made the tiniest of sighs, almost supported by a sound. Bob ruffled the dog's head and put his chipped enamel plate, with leftover gristle and gravy, on the floor. Mary jabbed her fork in Blackie's direction:

'That's why I've got a special mum's plate and you lot haven't. That dog has been licking his arse, his balls, and fuck knows what else all day. I like to know where my plate's been, thank you very much.'

Doll was having her tea at Mrs Harris's house, in sort of posh Woodford, Essex. She had been courting Len Harris since she was fourteen and planned to marry him as soon as possible.

'So where's Vi, then?' The words fell out of Bob, seemingly from nowhere. For twenty seconds the world spun on a different axis. Mary gave Bob a deaf look. Win and Robert made themselves busy clearing the table and left the room.

'I said, where's Vi?'

'Round her mate's house,' said Mary. She expertly rolled them two thin, thin smokes. Prison practice. As Mary started to talk about anything but Vi, Bob would speak of nothing else.

'Who is this mate? And where does she live? And has she been home at all? I've not seen her for days.' Sometimes Bob would answer his own queries. If there was a gap, Mary would fill it with 'I know' and 'mmm' and 'Tell me about it'.

Then he farted a symphony. She went into the scullery for his Milk of Magnesia and fed him a large spoonful; he looked at her as she wiped the whiteness from the corner of his mouth with the hem of her apron, and decided to say no more. She got his coat and off he went to the pub.

*

Mary, ready for bed in an old coat she used as a dressing gown, with her hair in two long plaits hanging down her back, heard the commotion before they were even inside the front door.

The thrashing and hollering carried on through the hallway and the living room, out to the scullery and back again. He had Vi's blonde perm in one hand and was smacking her with the other. Mary, trying to pull him off, got a punch in the eye. Vi bounced free and quickly walloped her dad half a dozen times round his head. As she was running out, shouting that she was never coming back – ever – Blackie bit her leg and then barked off, scared.

Mary and Bob were left alone with themselves, to assault each other with bile. He, tipsy and tired, stood lost on Uncle William's gift of a carpet. Mary sat at the table and rolled another smoke. Eventually he moved into the scullery and put Blackie out in the backyard.

She thought he was stroking her, asking her forgiveness.

Shnip. Shnip.

Crying, he placed the scissors and her two red plaits in front of her on the table and went to bed. She would never grow her hair again.

After they heard their father out for the count and snoring, Win and Robert said their prayers and allowed sleep to take them.

Vi. Where was Vi?

Mary sat up all night, listening to the house moaning at her. Bob went to work, the kids went to school, nobody spoke. Nobody mentioned the haircut, or Mum's black eye.

In the silence of the empty and unpleasant house, Mary heard the clatter of a swagger.

Vi.

Vi, her lovely green eyes smudged with yesterday's eye-black, in scuffed high heels and wearing a coat that had once been some kind of animal.

'It suits you,' she said, giving Mary's splayed, chopped hair and swollen, black and blue eye the once-over. 'He should have made that a pair, then at least it could look like make-up.'

'How did you get back in? When did you back get in?' Mary asked, pushing Vi's hands away.

'I never left, did I? I just slammed the front door and hid behind the coats on the rack till he went off to bed. Then I crept upstairs and slept in Doll's bed in case he woke up and started again. He wouldn't go into her room, would he? Anyway, let me tell you about this bloke.' Mary had always told all her girls that they were sitting on gold mines, and Vi had been mining. Out of her shabby handbag came stockings, chocolates, and some cheap scent.

Mary would have preferred the cash.

Boxing Day 1956

Why is it so hard to wee when your bum is cold?

To get to the lavatory you didn't have to go through the backyard any more, because Granddad had knocked a wonky doorway through from the outside wall at the end of the scullery, but it was still really an out-in-the-backyard type of lavatory. Going through the scullery might stop you getting wet or blown over in the wind but it didn't stop you getting cold. The wind blew under the big gap of the old back door and made the electric light swing and spray light over the frozen carcasses of stiff spiders.

Please let me wee.

Everyone could hear what you were doing in there, and if people were not whispering you could hear what was happening in the scullery. I thought maybe my piddle had frozen inside my body and that when it came out it would be an icicle or an iceberg. I thought of soft fluffy snow and hoped for the best. I could hear voices and the running of the tap, the stove door being opened, my mum laughing at something Aunt Doll had said. The smell of meat was juicing my spit.

Then I wee'd a hot burning tiddle, not an icicle or snowflake at all. It warmed me up and I decided to stay out of the way a while, hoping it was too cold for living spiders. I used to be able to pull their legs off and everything, so I have touched them, though only the skinny ones. I could hear invisible spiders thinking about me, and I thought about them.

'If a man laid a finger on me, I'm sorry, Doll, but that would be it.'

'They've all laid a bit more than a finger on the lot of us,' I heard Aunt Vi answer Mum.

I heard them all enjoy some sauciness. Mum, Nanny, Aunt Doll, and Aunt Vi were smacking plates, filling saucepans with water, and clinking knives and forks. Dinner wasn't too far off. It was obviously all systems go.

'No, I mean it, if my Bill were to have the gall even to raise his hand to me, that would be it. That's not what you call a man, so you might as well fuck off out of there.' Mum sounded pissed off, even though she had laughed at Aunt Vi. I thought, 'Fuck off out of where?' It sounded so exciting to fuck off out of there, as if there was another there than here.

CHAPTER SIX

Mary

Win and Robert had been at school in Becontree for six months and they liked it. Win told Robert that she had come top of the class in spelling and that her poem had been read out. Robert showed her his metalwork treasure. He had made a pair of tin bookends, shaped like garden gates, with a sunburst effect. They dawdled towards the school gates, laughing about what could you do with bookends when you don't have any books?

With 'Ta-ta's and 'See you tomorrow's, Win and Robert weaved through the other kids onto the street. Robert whistled for Blackie. Someone whistled back, then an 'Oi!' Turning round they saw their mother with the coalman and the coalman's lorry. It was piled high with the guts of their house.

'Move yourselves, get on.'

They were hoiked onto the back in exactly the same way as when they had arrived in Becontree Heath.

'Where's Blackie?' Robert asked the world.

'Win, we're going to drop you off at the station. Wait for your dad and give him this,' Mary handed Win a piece of butcher's paper with an address on it.

'Doll is staying at Mrs Harris's again tonight, so you'll have to meet her at work tomorrow and let her know what's afoot.'

Win had a good idea what was afoot, but kept quiet.

'Where's Blackie? What's happening?' asked Robert, bending and twisting his tin bookends into scrap.

'He's with Vi at our new house. Stop whining.' Mary jumped into the passenger seat and they were off. At least it wasn't raining.

Win waited at the station for her dad, and thought of the wallop she'd get when he read the piece of paper telling him they were on the move again, as there was no Doll to protect her. She tried to remember the poem she'd written, the poem that she'd read out, the poem that was about Garwobs, the ghost in the mirror – but it all disentangled in her nine-year-old head.

> He watches you when you're combing your hair
> Garwobs, Garwobs, lives in guess where?
> Don't stay too long looking at you
> Or suddenly his face will start coming through.
> Nanny says he is beauty's ghost . . .

By the time Bob walked out of the station, she had decided the poem was crap and the class must have been taking the piss out of her.

A silent Bob and a scrunched-up Win got the train to Stratford. If Eaton Place, Belgravia, was the most expensive area in London, then Heaton Place, Stratford, even with its la-di-da 'H', was the cheapest.

Back to the East End.

'I was frightened out there in the wilds of nowhere, all on me own.' Mary was playing for the sympathy vote.

'You didn't pay the fucking rent, did you?'

Bob was mooching around the geography of their new hovel. Robert and Win were trying to find the dog. Vi was in the backyard having a crafty roll-up. And there was Flo, ordered to take a day off work and help. She had asked her Granny Clara what she should do, but the old girl just clacked her gums and looked sad. Flo must have taken that as some kind of command, because she took the day off work.

Heaton Place gave them the same number of rooms as they had had in Becontree, only everything was smaller, smellier, damper. The lavatory was outside in the backyard, along with a zinc bath hanging on a huge hook in the wall. The previous tenants had gone up in the world: the father to Wormwood Scrubs, the four kids under five to Dr Barnardo's, and the mother resting quietly in West Ham cemetery.

Mary got her tribe scrubbing bleach into every crevice, hoping that TB couldn't linger in floorboards and brickwork. Most of the walls had the blood smears of squashed bugs. She needed green paint – green gloss paint would frighten the bugs away. Within two days the four bedrooms, the narrow passage, the stairway, the scullery, and the front room – everywhere – shone with apple-coloured walls. The house was so damp it took a week to dry, and not one of them had survived without green paint on some part of their hair and clothes. The bugs never came back.

Mary was a verbal acrobat. Leaping and cavorting lies into possible truths:

'That bastard put the rent up without telling me; it was an excuse to get us out, wasn't it? When he asked me for the back money, he knew I didn't have it. So there we are. I'm sorry, Bob, but I'm doing my best – put the kettle on, Win, make your dad a cup of tea – and then it dawned on me, fuck him, I thought, he's done us all a favour, this is nearer to your work, nearer to your mum's, at least I know people round here, shops and all that. I know it don't look much now, but once I've got me curtains up, cleaned the windows and that ...'

She broke down a bit then. Bob looked at her, remembering her lovely hair. Win nervously handed him a cracked cup of tea. He handed it to Mary and went out to find a pub.

Blackie was never seen again. He should never have bitten Vi.

Boxing Day 1956

The so-called half-hour before dinner was up was a very long half-hour. Everyone was aggravated. Black Gary, Little George, and Barbara were jumping and jiving upstairs to Elvis Presley. Nanny was shouting up to them to turn it off; Mum and Aunt Doll were trying to shut Nanny up or she'd wake the boys. Why did everyone have to shout? Both Lionel and Buster were spark-out on the bed in the other room, and we didn't need any more noise to join in. I couldn't hear myself think.

Ron had come down and we were playing the spelling game. I was saving up the word 'asphalt' for the last minute. Then I'd have him. Hardly anybody knew how to spell 'asphalt'. Aunt Doll and Mum were coming in and out, laying the table, followed by Aunt Flo, who kept getting under their feet.

'Flo, go upstairs, get them to calm down and turn that bloody music off. After that you can come and play with Ron and Rob,' Aunt Doll said to her.

Ron and I looked at each other, our faces like empty plates, 'Oh, no, not Aunt Flo.'

Last year we didn't do Boxing Day, we came over on New Year's Eve instead. All the grown-ups went to the pub and Aunt Flo was supposed to be baby-sitting. We did horrible things to her – even I was scared. She had pissed herself right in front of us. I wondered whether Ron was thinking the same thing. It was Big George's fault, he'd started it.

'I'll get some some more coal, then I'll come and play,' she said.

Flo was quite good at spelling. She wrote really slowly, which was a bit boring for Ron and me.

The cousins had got fed up and came back downstairs. Seeing us with Aunt Flo, playing with pens and paper, they left us to it and charged along to the scullery to get in the way and get told off. The smell of roasting food mixed with hunger was getting us all a little bit humpy and I thought the ruckus going on in the scullery would wake my baby brothers any minute. Right now I didn't want to be interrupted.

I'd won a point with 'asphalt' – not even Aunt Flo knew that one.

She got her own back though.

Ron had smirked when she'd whispered it, so he must have come across it before. Why did she whisper it?

'Intercourse.'

I pictured the letters and never forgot them after that.

CHAPTER SEVEN

Flo

F lo was a few months older than she thought she was. Probably nobody ever did put her straight about that. She was born in 1918, not 1919. Her mum and dad got married some time afterwards. No one put her straight about that either.

Flo lived in the distance. Her five senses were individually perfect, but clashing together they created cow-like confusion. She liked to be given orders, told what to do. She liked her baby sister Doll coming downstairs for a cuddle and a kiss on the front step. She liked helping her Granny Clara with the washing up. She liked Uncle William telling her words she'd never heard of. She cared about the Chinaman. He knew her every thought before she had it.

Coming from a tribe with a lot to say for themselves, Flo was the oddity. No one could remember her voice, her sound. When she did speak, it was either drowned out by the noise of others or simply ignored, as if nothing had happened. Granny and Uncle William didn't mean to, but even they did it from time to time. Her secret life downstairs of decent food, clean, ironed clothes, even a few toys, caused jealousy from the menagerie upstairs, and when they moved out they mostly forgot about her.

All except Doll.

Flo would visit the family from time to time, depending on the difficulty of the journey and whether or not Doll was around. Doll was staying more and more at Len's mother's house now that she had got engaged, and Flo would sometimes meet her there. That was a night out.

Whatever happened to the others, Flo was safe with Granny. Clara would take her wages off her and give her money each day to get to work, saving the rest to buy her nice frocks and shoes. Flo scrubbed up well, she was tall with a good figure, she had pretty, light-brown hair and clear skin. Her big, mournful, grey-green eyes curtained an empty space.

Of course, she would find herself a boyfriend.

They said war was coming.

The war seemed to dribble in with a health warning, then out again.

Meanwhile Mary, at the age of thirty-nine, popped out another daughter – another sister for Flo, with twenty-one years between them.

The war came back, this time with muscles.

Flo thought the war meant that the music had stopped and now only chatter could come out of the wireless – or maybe that her dad had not fixed it right.

'Why do I have to leave Lyons Corner House and make tents. I don't know where it is and I only know the number fifteen bus. How do I get there? Who told them about me? Have I done something wrong again?'

The excitement of the Underground and tea cups and ladies in hats became a long walk to the tent factory where she didn't know anyone. The liquorice bite of engine oil mixed with the cobwebby, snuffy smell of dry canvas seemed to smoke her nostrils. The wireless was on all day in the factory but could only be heard between the whirr and clack of heavy machinery. After a while she forgot about it and got on with making the tents. The comforting aroma of chicory coffee and sugary fondants was now only a half-cocked memory. Doll tried to explain that everyone who was not going to war had to change jobs and muck in.

'I mean, look at me, I hate working at Tate and Lyle's, but that's where they've put me.'

'Does that mean we'll get more sugar if the Germans win?'

'It's very complicated, Flo, don't worry about it.'

'Granny said I'm not really making tents but little houses and Uncle William says that makes me an architect, which is important, but it's not that difficult. So why has Vi gone to Suffolk to pick vegetables and have a holiday?'

'Be grateful for small mercies,' said Doll.

Flo never could conquer the gas mask, so the rest of the family left her to it and hoped for the best. The war had now started with a vengeance and she would find the shop on the corner, or the scruffy house in the middle, which had been there in the morning, gone by home time. It confused her and she'd get lost. Bombs flew around her like flies round shit, but she would get the message four beats behind everyone else. People would drag her down the Underground, under stairs, into all sorts of places that she started to believe Hitler knew her personally, that he had been watching her, like the Chinaman, and that it was all her fault.

Pat Jones manned the ARP depot in Sebart Road, not far from the tent factory. A soft, lonely man, ten years older than Flo. After a few months of chatting, kissing, and fiddling, they got engaged.

'Well, he's no oil painting, but if he wants to take you on, good luck to him,' Uncle William told her. Clara kept her cards close to her chest. The rest of the family, in dribs and drabs, got to give him the once-over. They were all in agreement: 'What an ugly bastard.' From then on he was called 'Cyclops'. He and Flo didn't seem to mind.

They had a poverty-stricken wedding at the town hall, with

no cake and no photos, and went back to live with Clara and Uncle William. The bombs rained down and always managed to miss their house. Mary Roberts was not so lucky – or maybe she was. A few windows got blown out, a back lavatory was hit. She was on the move more than usual, but the war was kind to her: no one died and no one got paid.

Flo found Uncle William dead in the front room. She hadn't gone to work owing to the headache that had kept her awake all night and she was in the house by herself. Clara had got the early bus to Stratford to try and find some fresh fish. Flo called his name, then she called on the Chinaman: 'Why are you blue? Why is he blue?' She whirling-dervished around.

It was the money that stopped everything. Trying to stop herself from bouncing around, she had grabbed the wooden handles of the two drawers of the sideboard and managed to pull them right out, spilling their contents all over the place. Wads of white five-pound notes tied together with brown string saw daylight.

Money – Mum.

That's how her tin plate deciphered the scene for her: get Mum. She would tell her about Uncle William and to prove it she would take the money.

Clara knew something was up the minute she turned the corner and saw an ambulance.

'Sit down, Mum, it's bad,' Mary said to her. 'I've sent Flo to go and get Bob and Doll. I'll make you a cuppa when the doctor's finished.' The doctor and the ambulance men removed the body and the two women stared at the scene of the crime.

'It was our Flo. She found him and then went berserk, apparently, you know how she can be. I'll put the kettle on, the others will be here soon.' Mary moved into the scullery and left her mother-in-law in the front room with her grief.

Flo was in such a state by the time she got to the Tate and Lyle factory. It had taken her half an hour to get there. She wet herself. Doll knew something important was going on; she slapped Flo's face and then managed to translate. It took another half-hour to get to Bob's work, so by the time the three of them got back they had missed the going of Uncle William, brother William. Bachelor of this parish.

'Heart attack? He was only fifty,' Bob mumbled to the Chinaman.

Mary cuddled her mother-in-law into her bosom, Doll cleared up, and Flo was sent into the scullery to make more tea. She stared at the open bag of Tate and Lyle's sugar, all damp and crusty round the edges, and thought of Germans.

'How much was the quack? Where's his bill?'

'Don't worry your mum about that now, Bob,' said Mary, rolling a smoke for herself.

Flo was moving in and out of the front room, bringing in the tea. One cup at a time. On the last trip . . .

'How much was it?' he pushed. He was trying to imagine life without William, he was trying to imagine how much a death cost in hard cash. Mary licked the fag paper and pondered on those secret bundles of fivers that Flo had given her. She didn't have to worry too long about her answer, although it was a heart-stopping moment for a second:

'I didn't count any of it, honest, they just flew at me and he was all blue and the Chinaman was looking at us all and I looked for Granny in the cupboard . . .' Before Flo could complete her mangled story, she went up on her toes, arched her back, and fell like lightning onto the lino. Her back arched again, she gurgled, her body reverberated like a motorbike ticking over, her eyes rolled backwards into Flo-land, a white froth oozed through her bared teeth, and piss ran down her legs. Doll forced her mouth open and wedged her purse between her teeth so she couldn't bite off her tongue.

Mary was wishing that she had done – maybe one day.

'This is all we fucking need,' slipped out from someone in the room.

Bob looked at his two daughters, looked at his mother, and was lost at sea. Mary decided to think for all of them, and he was very, very grateful.

'I've got to get back to the baby, Bob, I left her next door. Doll, you stay here, I'll get back as soon as.'

'No. I'll see to Carol and take Flo with me, she needs some fresh air and a walk before she has her big sleep. When Cyclops gets back, tell him where she is. I'll phone Len and let him know what's what', said Doll.

Flo held on to her sister's hand to begin the long, wobbly, forty-minute walk. She felt tired. She felt, she felt – not much. Trying to break through this heavy gauze, trying to unstop the sound of the ocean in her ears. She felt as if she was behind the huge screen at the pictures. *Now Voyager*, Bette Davis saying over and over again, 'Why ask for the moon . . .'

While Doll was in the phone box, Flo tapped on the window to her, smiled, and gave the thumbs-up.

'God's cleaning my windows, I think I'll be all right now. Bit tired, though.'

Doll put her in Win and Robert's empty room. They were still evacuated in Cornwall. Flo slept a full twenty-four hours in her epileptic grave. Pat Jones snuck in beside her and didn't go to work for a few days. Then he took her back home to help the family with the funeral arrangements.

Who was going to pay for it? How was it going to be paid for? Was Uncle William insured? Going through his things seemed to create more mysteries than it solved. Flo listened to all this and thought about the bundle of fivers. She watched her mother watching everyone else, taking the temperature of the room.

'What about all that money I found, Mum?'

For the first time in her life, everyone stopped in their tracks at the sound of her voice. Flo froze. Then they all looked at Mary.

'What?'

'What are you on about, Flo?' asked Bob.

The air-raid warning whined into their ears. They scattered to their favourite bolt holes. Bob dragged his mum down the shelter, Pat Jones pulled Flo under the stairs. Mary stayed where she was and took her chances.

Eventually the all-clear sounded. For Mary as well as for London.

'I told you she found his money, but you were all too upset to take my meaning. I've got it here – not let it out of my sight, have I? Put the kettle on, Flo, there's a good girl.' Mary rooted around in her shopping bag. Flo and Pat Jones went to make the tea. Clara went out into the street to see if her neighbours and their dwellings were still upright. Mary handed over four white fivers tied up with string. Just in case the string got mentioned. Flo heard her dad say, 'Well, at least it'll cover the funeral.' She thought of all those fivers, all that string, all that money, and realized they were going to give Uncle William a right royal send-off.

'Blimey, if this little funeral cost all of Uncle William's money, how much must the old King's have cost?' Flo thought to herself as she walked in the pouring rain to West Ham cemetery. Bob was holding on to Clara, two of her brothers followed behind them, then came Doll and Len with Mary, Len holding the big black umbrella. Flo dawdled behind and got herself soaked.

Win and Robert were still in Cornwall and Vi wasn't there either because she'd gone AWOL. Two-year-old Carol was left in the care of Mrs Balkwell.

Doll inherited the Chinaman.

After her William died, Clara Roberts aged a hundred years.

Flo did her best to look after her, but cooking and cleaning was a mystery without the orders to go with it. Pat Jones did most of it in the end.

Two years later Flo fell pregnant.

So did Mary, again. At forty-three, without even trying. It was quite complicated to explain to Clara – and to Flo herself – which baby would be an uncle or an aunt, which a nephew or a niece.

Mary gave birth to her last baby, George. Flo gave birth to her first, she called her Pattie. George was the uncle, Pattie the niece and Mary and Bob's first grandchild.

Bombs dropped, babies howled, Clara gave in and died.

With Granny gone, Flo felt, well, not much really. She always looked as if she was waiting for a bus.

Vi was on the run for something or other and had gone into hiding in Aldgate. Then out of the blue she turned up, though she wasn't supposed to. Flo was a bit on edge, knowing that her dad had told them all never to see or speak to Vi again. Mary started visiting as well. It took a while before it dawned on Flo that her place was being used as a secret meeting hole for Mary and Vi to run a little business. Vi would have stockings, tobacco, and chocolates, and in return Mary would flog Vi curtains and linens; sometimes they would just do a straight swap. It didn't take too long before Flo wanted to be enjoying herself with Vi in Aldgate, with Mary taking charge of little Pattie round at hers. Mary told Bob that Flo had got herself a job. Eventually, Flo stayed in Aldgate, Pat Jones was abandoned, and his little girl was brought up with the rest of the kids at Mary and Bob's. He got to see her once a week. He had to pay for the privilege.

It had been exciting being in Aldgate: the men, the pubs, the Americans, the money. When Vi fell pregnant and decided to stay where she was, with a Bengali merchant seaman, Flo was

out on her ear. No more Granny Roberts, no more Uncle
William, no Pat Jones. So she went back to her mum and dad's,
and Pattie. The little rented house in Plaistow was full, so she
had to sleep where she could, which was mostly with Mary
when Bob was on nights. Three small bedrooms upstairs and a
front parlour downstairs had to comfort eight bodies. Bob,
Mary, Flo, eighteen-year-old Win, sixteen-year-old Robert,
seven-year-old Carol, and the candle-nosed, snotty toddlers,
George and Pattie.

It was 1946.

'Get off, she's not wearing a pair of my drawers. I don't know
where she's been.'

'Oh, shut up, Win, for fuck's sake, else you'll wake the old
man. I'll give her a pair of his underpants.'

Mary would find jobs for Flo, moving her about if another job
paid a farthing more, and would make her run around at home.
Pat Jones would call once a week to see Pattie, and Flo would try
and get extra money out of him – when she was there. She had
a tendency to disappear for days on end. Asked what she'd been
up to, she'd just say, 'What you on about? I've been here all the
time.'

Boxing Day 1956

A great banging on the front door and shouts through the letter-box told us that Big George was back. Thrown out from his mate's house and sent home to have his dinner with his own family. My uncle George.

'I'll go,' I shouted to anyone who wanted to hear.

All the grown-ups were fiddling about with food in the scullery, apart from Aunt Flo, who was getting in everyone's way, mooching backwards and forwards down the passage with knives and forks, mint sauce, pepper and salt. I was so excited at the homecoming of Big George that I tripped her up on my way to the front door and that put the kibosh on the mint sauce. It missed me, but Flo got covered in the vinegary green slimy bits. I knew it would be a great show when I opened the door.

'Ugh, Flo, where's your hankie? Your face is covered in snot. Clean yourself up, you dozy mare.'

We both sneered at her and she attempted to cuff him round the head at the same time as getting herself upright. He ducked so fast that her hand crunched against wall and she burst into tears.

The commotion brought Nanny and Aunt Vi into the passage. But George was already rushing towards the scullery and food and I highjumped after him. He was five years older than me, and the only one in the entire world that I wanted to impress. I wanted to be as dangerous, as funny, as brave. My mum and aunts spoilt him even though they knew he ran Nanny ragged – or maybe because of it.

'Whatever have I done to deserve you? What bastard up there decided to punish me like this? You'll be the fucking death of me,' Nanny would wail.

George would then start wailing, taking the piss out of her. His sisters would join in and the cat's chorus would make Nanny's face fold up, her mouth and eyes tightly shut, as she found somewhere to perch – surrendering.

It was always Aunt Doll who turned it into a different game.

'Aye-aye-aye, I love you ve-r-r-r-r-r-y much ...' she started singing in a funny voice and wiggling her hips. Her arms were waving above her head, with a spoon in one hand and the carving knife in the other. Then Mum and Aunt Vi joined in. The cousins tumbled down from upstairs to see what the hoo-ha was all about. Everyone 'aye-aye'-ed around the scullery, apart from me and Black Gary. He peeled away and retraced his steps upstairs while I made my way to the front room to see what Buster was up to.

Walking down the passage I saw that Aunt Flo was still snivelling in the same place where we had left her, and I could hear the cousins 'aye-aye'-ing their way back upstairs, doing the conga line. I found Buster looking through Pattie's hair. She didn't seem to mind. He was copying what he'd seen Mum do to me once a week: the nit trail.

The scullery singing stopped as quickly as it had started, followed by loud, chesty laughter. Flo had returned.

'You're enough to put anyone off their dinner at the best of times, Flo. Can't you even walk in a straight line?' Aunt Vi was actually trying to be nice. I knew that because she had an 'I give up' sound to her voice.

'Go to the pub. No, go to the pub, for Christ's sake.' Nanny was back on form. 'I'm not dishing anything up until they are all here.'

Hunger must have made George do as he was told, and he went to the pub.

Five of us were in the scullery eating our dinner off the bath top. Big George sat at one end on a wooden crate; the rest of us had to kneel on the lino. I was next to George, Black Gary next to me, then Little George, and finally Pattie at the horrible end – the tap end. The taps didn't work, but Granddad hadn't bothered to take them off. Pattie had to raise her arms and dive down to stab at her food. She looked like a lonely vulture about to take flight.

Ron and Barbara were allowed to eat their food in the front room with the grown-ups.

We all munched as quickly as possible; although the room was hot from all the hours of cooking, our skinny knees cracked under us on the hard floor. Little George was the only one who could eat and rapid-fire chat at the same time. He didn't waste a crumb, no sprays of half-chewed food escaped from him, just sneaky words: 'Makes a change from all that rice' or 'Wait till you see the bike that Mum got me. It's a bit big at the mo, but I can still ride it.'

Black Gary didn't have a bike, and I wondered what he had got for Christmas. I was quite pleased with my presents: one Potato Man kit and two huge jigsaw puzzles. My stocking always had, every year, a drawing pad, coloured pencils, oranges, and nuts. I wanted a dressing-up doll, but my mum 'didn't believe in them'. She didn't want me to have girly things. She'd say, 'You'll have enough of all that once you're grown up,' when I whined for a toy kitchen set with a little iron and ironing board.

I could hear the men in the front room laughing and chaffing, and I felt jealous that Ron and Barbara were in there, on proper chairs. Big George had found where the beer was kept out in the backyard and had opened a bottle, which he shared with Little George. There'd be ructions if they were found out. I swapped a slice of lamb and my Yorkshire pudding for two of Pattie's potatoes and ate them with my fingers on the way to the front room. Buster was asleep on Mum's lap, having shared her dinner, and everyone was smoking.

'Look at her and her spuds. It's the only thing I can guarantee to get down her. Have you come in to help clear the table, Rob?' I hadn't but I knew that Mum wasn't asking me, she was telling me.

I looked at Granddad. His eyes were all watery and red and he was nodding at me to go to him. I looked around the dinner table, not at the faces but at where their hands were. Their hands told me no one was in a hurry to move, so I went and sat on Granddad's lap.

'Do you read the Bible, Rob?' he whispered in my ear.

I whispered back, 'Only in bits at school assembly and on a Friday morning when we have to go down the church.'

'Well, do you know that monkeys are as much God's children as the rest of us? They're clever, very clever. So clever that they've worked out that although they can speak English, and even Hindustani some of them, they know they're better off keeping shtum. Do you know why?'

I shook my head and knew he was about to tell me something very important. 'Because they know that if they let on, they would be put to work like the rest of us. Here you see before you a table of monkeys who couldn't keep their fucking mouths shut.' His voice was louder now and I knew he was using me to talk to everyone else.

'He's off,' said Aunt Vi. Nanny smiled a silent code to the others. Mum looked on edge. My dad looked sleepy and was grinning outside of himself. He was somewhere else.

'I knew a monkey very well once. Knew him in a personal

way – all his little pleasures and tricks – and he knew mine. He was more than a pal to me. He understood everything I said. Everything that was going on. Are you listening to me?'

I nodded again, but could feel that Granddad was changing from a cheerful mood to an unknown one.

'Now, who do you reckon, Rob, around this table, could and would do harm to my best pal?'

'Oh, for fuck's sake, Bob, don't start on that again.' Nanny had finished her fag and was scraping the dinner leavings on to one plate.

'Mary, I'm going for a bit of shut-eye on your bed, if that's all right with you?' my dad said to Nanny.

'Make room for me, Bill,' said Uncle Len, and the two of them dotted out their fags and moved into the back room. I hoped they wouldn't crush our Lionel. Uncle Korim was already asleep, but he was quite happy doing it sitting down at the table.

Nanny and Aunt Flo did my job with the plates and left the room calling out to Pattie to come and give a hand. Mum, Aunt Doll, and Aunt Vi all stared at the tablecloth.

'This monkey, my companion in many lonely months away from home ... not only watched over me and my belongings, but would crack nuts for me, pour me a bowl of water to sluice my face in, was my alarm clock ... oh, my little darling ... he was everything ... my own personal valet, as if I were a king.'

I was wondering about 'valet' when Granddad burst into tears. I looked at Mum, who looked at Aunt Doll. I could tell they didn't know what to do, so they both looked at Aunt Vi, who was grinning.

'He's pissed, he'll have conked out in a minute,' she told them.

'Ron, Barbara, upstairs. Go on, get round that electric fire while we clear up down here.' Aunt Doll had decided she wasn't going to take a chance on what might come out next.

'My monkey protected me from all the blights of life. He would have died for me, and me for him. And d'you know what? He did die for me in a way. That wicked old cow got rid of him. To this day I don't know how, but she did. Anything I've ever loved, she's destroyed. Anything.'

Before anyone could say anything about his tears, Nanny came back in. She had heard the last bit.

'Best pal? You poor bastard, is that the best you could do? I did you a favour. Go and have a lie down, you silly old git,' she said.

She came close to us and cupped her hand to his mouth. I looked at her hand; it seemed to hang in front of his face for a very long time. Her hand. A big cloutable hand. I could see her stubby fingernails as they curled inwards towards her broad palms. I thought of elephants' feet. Eventually he gave in and flopped his false teeth into her hand.

'We don't need another turn-out like last night, do we? You go and sleep off your gutful of hops and I'll put these back in to soak. Go on, go and put your head down upstairs.' Nanny sounded forgiving. I looked over to the aunts. They were all staring at each other, trying to avoid looking at the teeth business.

Granddad didn't budge and neither did I. Nanny tut-tutted and stomped back out to the scullery. Mum put the sleeping Buster in the old armchair by the fire and told me to keep an eye on him, and left the room, followed by Aunt Doll and Aunt Vi.

Without disturbing the dribbling, snoozing Uncle Korim, I went to my sideboard and from the left-hand top drawer brought out the heavy black book with the shiny gold pages. Granddad shuffled to the armchair opposite Buster and waited for me to climb onto his lap.

CHAPTER EIGHT

Doll

'She was some old tom, I reckon. She looked like one, but isn't he beautiful? The dad was a Yank, they think. We've called him Ron.' Doll was crying and laughing into the little bundle in her arms.

'How much was he?' asked Mary.

Doll gave her mother a look that could perish concrete. After six years of trying to get pregnant, with a few quid here and a few fibs there, she had adopted this sweet blob of a baby. She would change his life.

'He looks a bit of a Jew-boy to me. Has he been circumcised?'

'You fucking wicked old cow, can't you be happy for me for once? I couldn't care less if he had horns and a cloven hoof, he's still mine. And I'll make sure you don't have a hand in any part of him.'

Six years earlier, Doll had been in a different state of high excitement.

'Fancy being my bridesmaid, Flo?'

'Oh, yeah! Not half. But where will you live?'

'With Mrs Harris. Me and Len can have the big room upstairs, and it's safer out at Woodford than round here.'

'Are you having a baby?'

'Not yet, Flo, give us a chance. The old man would skin me and Len alive if that happened.'

Something else happened, though. It was a big something –
and it was definitely something to do with Mary.

One week to go before her wedding and Doll had just won a
'Who Looks Like Katharine Hepburn?' contest at the factory.
Her mates were coming round for the evening to look at all her
engagement presents and the things she and Len had saved up
and bought for themselves. Their linen came from Mary, of
course, but they had had to pay her for it. The wedding dress
wasn't quite finished, so they couldn't see *that*. The night before,
Uncle William and Granny Roberts had given her a beautiful
vase and she had put it in the wardrobe with the rest of her
things. The girls laughed when they saw the padlock on the
wardrobe.

'You don't know my mother.'

Pinned into the lining of Doll's coat was the key. Many times
a day she would check it was still there.

'You don't know my mother.'

After a fiddle and a faddle she unlocked the wardrobe, and
pinned the key back inside her coat. With a 'Dah, dah!' and a
curtsy, she opened the door.

The room changed colour.

'She's fucking Houdini,' mumbled Doll, barely hitting the
consonants.

Everyone stared into the completely empty wardrobe. There
was lots of 'She must have another key' and 'Maybe she got it
out of your coat when you were asleep,' until Maud, Doll's best
friend since school, said, 'She didn't need the key, Doll, she's
taken the back off the wardrobe.'

Not even Doll could laugh this one away. The other girls went
quiet. Maud lit a fag and slipped it to her. Two big tears made an
appearance for a second. Doll tossed her head and forced them
back where they had come from.

Bob walked into the house to Doll and her mates marching

out, with an 'And you'll never see me again, so don't you even dare come looking.'

From that moment, she lived at Len's. Got married from Len's. The day before the wedding, a letter arrived in Mary's handwriting. Doll didn't open it straight away, she had to get to work. She knew what it would be. A begging, I'm sorry, you have no idea what I've been going through, snot-rag kind of a letter. She didn't need it. She was still livid.

It took ages to get to the Tate and Lyle factory from Woodford, and she had to do a large part of the journey on foot. It gave her time to badger herself about the wedding the next day. She hadn't spoken to the family since the wardrobe debacle. Would Mum even turn up? she wondered. As long as her Dad gave her away, and Flo was the bridesmaid, it would have to do.

Doll punched her card and clocked in for work, was just about to take her coat off, when the siren went. 'Get moving.' The whole factory went to the shelters. People were undecided whether to sit down, stay standing, or form a queue. They might not be down there long. Someone started singing, and Doll attempted a tap-dance, then did a turn as Carmen Miranda, piling a bunch of woolly gloves on her head and trying to keep them there. Everyone else flopped down and wedged in where they could. They were down there a long time. A hot, sweet stench tried to insinuate its way into them. Was it bodies? A new kind of gas? It all went quiet.

'I'm getting married tomorrow, do you think Hitler will leave me some guests?'

'Don't worry, Doll, he's only after your Mum,' shouted out Maud.

The all-clear sounded.

They couldn't believe their eyes, or their noses.

From Silvertown all the way down to the Woolwich Ferry, the streets were ablaze with burning sugar. As if a toffee-apple volcano had erupted. Firemen, bells, police, ARP wardens. Tate and Lyle had taken a direct hit.

Everyone said their own version of 'Better get home, let them know I'm all right.' Doll and Maud cadged a lift from a butcher's van. Doll jumped out near Stratford, but it would take Maud almost to her front door, if she still had one.

Doll stood on the corner of her mum's road, saw it was all still standing, and walked on, hoping she hadn't been spotted. Granny Roberts and Uncle William lived half a dozen streets away, so she moved on to there. That was all as it should be. She told them she couldn't stay long, otherwise Len would be sending out a search party for her, but she'd have a cup of tea and tell them all about the inferno of treacle on its way to the Ferry.

She decided to open Mary's letter.

Dear Doris,

I do hope you're pleased with yourself, showing us up like that in front of all your workmates. You've created ructions here with the old man, upset the kids, and I don't know what's what. The trouble you've caused your mother may never be able to be unravelled this time. All over what? A few bits and bobs, and most of those I supplied. Well, my girl, you can go and fuck yourself. I've had enough of you. You won't see me or the old man at the wedding, and I'm not letting the kids come either. May God strike you down before you manage to reach the vicar.

I hope it fucking rains pellets on the lot of you.

Mum.

Uncle William gave her away, Flo was a lovely bridesmaid, and Granny Clara stood at the back, behind the Harrises, looking sad and defeated. None of the others could have come anyway. Win and Robert were still in Cornwall, and Vi had gone

AWOL. Photographs were taken of the little group, of Doll and Len on their own, and there was a special one of the wedding cake when they got back to Woodford. The three-tiered cake was put on a trestle table out in the back garden. There was the usual photo of the bride and groom pretending to cut the cake, though in this instance they couldn't have done anything else since the tall, beautifully decorated cake, with its little bride and groom on top, was made entirely of cardboard. There was a real cake inside, a small jam-filled Victoria sponge that Mrs Harris had made.

Six months later Uncle William had given himself away to oblivion, dead at fifty.

Once Flo had got over her fit and Doll had got her back to Mary's house without too much incident, she had given her some water and put her to bed. What had Flo been going on about? What money? Had she found Uncle William's money? Flo had given it to Mum, she'd said, loads of bundles of fivers tied with string. If she had given it to Mary, it would be there somewhere.

Doll went on the rummage. She turned out every cupboard, drawer, under this, over that. Not a whiff of it. So Doll sat down and wrote letters to Win and Robert in Cornwall about what had happened to Uncle William. She asked young Robert to look after his sister, as Win would take the going of her uncle especially badly. She didn't know where Vi was, so she couldn't do anything about that. Uncle William hadn't liked Vi anyway.

This funeral was cheap and uncheerful though Mary had gone to the trouble of supplying all the mourners with black outfits. Doll had thought this was another fine linen and curtains moment. Posh bandages to cover the weeping sores. She thought of Flo and Uncle William's money. According to Mary, he only left four large, white five-pound notes.

Back at the house, the talk was of his leavings. Did Clara Roberts want to keep the house as it was? Bob kept William's ring and Bible; he didn't want his clothes as they would be too big for him, so Pat Jones inherited those.

'Here, Doris, I know he always wanted you to have this,' said old Mrs Roberts.

The Chinaman.

Doll couldn't believe it. She remembered all those years ago when it used to haunt Mary in her dreams.

'Take it away with you today, there's a good girl.'

'They're real ivory, them teeth, Doll,' said Mary.

'Yes, I know, Mum. You don't mind me having it, Flo, do you?'

She had two rooms to choose from at Woodford. The Chinaman went from the bedroom to the front room, next week back to the bedroom; finally, when she got so wrapped up in her trying to have a baby state, it stayed where she had last left it, in the bedroom.

'Pregnant? You?' Doll stared at Mary in disbelief.

This was hard for Doll. She was spending tears and money on doctors, complicated tests, and generally being manhandled, with still no baby for her.

'You sure it's not just wind, Mum?'

'That's what I suggested to the doctor, or the change of life. When he said I was pregnant, I laughed. What? At forty-three? Anyway, my husband has been away for the past eighteen months.'

'But Dad hasn't been away.'

'I know he fucking hasn't, I was just testing the doctor's wherewithal.'

'Mum, what must he have thought? Not very nice for Dad, lying like that,' said Doll.

'Saucy bastard said it must be the Immaculate Conception

then, and I'd got the right name for it, Mary. I felt like chinning him.'

Doll washed little Carol's face and hands and put on the new frock she'd bought her. From the moment Carol was born Doll had spoilt her.

'Do you want to come and stay with me and Len at the weekend, darling?' Carol looked at Mary, who gave a nod.

So, as often as she could, Carol would stay in Woodford and be dressed in pretty frocks, and Doll and Len could play at being mum and dad. Every weekend they would go camping with their mates, Maud and George, in Chingford. George and Len, and Doll and Maud, had been friends since school. George had been Doll's first boyfriend, and Len had been Maud's; when they realized they had got it all the wrong way round, they swapped partners and lived happyish ever after. Occasionally, Doll would find it hard that her best friends couldn't stop breeding while she was finding it so hard to start. Carol was taught to swim, put up tents, and eat food over a fire in the dark, with help from Maud's two little girls.

'Why didn't Mum give me to you when I was first born? Then you wouldn't have to keep seeing the doctor, would you?'

'Because I didn't ask, I suppose. If I'd known what I know now, I would've done, darling, don't you worry.'

In the end, Doll talked to someone at Dr Barnardo's. After checking that she and Len weren't mass-murderers, and kept a clean house, they introduced her to Ada. Ada was living in a mother-and-baby house in Chelsea. She had a son she didn't need or want. Doll lived on pins for the next couple of months. First she could have him, then she couldn't, then maybe. Ada thought she could make a few bob by putting Doll through the wringer. Doll had been brought up by Mary Burke, and bided her time. After the adoption papers were finalized, Ada made the mistake of turning up at Woodford again, asking for more money. Doll threw a chamberpot of piss over her and threatened to call the police. Ada went out of their lives for ever and in came baby Ron.

Carol was only a little bit put out.

Her life in Woodford with its genteel poverty was the sweetest Doll had known. Len worked as a butcher in North London, Mr and Mrs Harris downstairs were easy enough to jog along with, and there was camping at the weekends. Doll enjoyed her first little garden, not only for drying the washing, but also for learning about flowers. Every Friday this *Watch with Mother* idyll would be interrupted with a visit to Punishment House, to see Mary and Bob and, hopefully, some of the others.

Turning the corner into Salmen Road, Doll could see Flo's little Pattie sitting on the doorstep picking her nose.

'Where's your Mum?'

Pattie would give a shrug and continue her concentrated digging; like her mother, she never spoke much.

'She's on the missing list again,' Mary shouted from indoors.

They hadn't even got the kettle on when a man in a cheap suit walked right in, bold as brass. He'd come for his money, which, of course, Mary didn't have. No one put up a fight. Doll found half a crown and he was pacified.

'"Nanny says she's not in" wouldn't have worked today, would it, Mary? Should've kept your front door shut.' With that he left.

'Sapphi-eyed old bastard. Sorry about that, Doll, I'll give it you back next week. Or you can have this lovely pair of sheets I've got.'

Doll chose the sheets.

'Is Vi coming?'

'She can't, she's doing six months in Beaconsfield.'

'What for?'

'Don't ask me, Doll, you know what a lying little cow she can be. Oh, and she's pregnant. Which, knowing her, may or may not be true. For Christ's sake, don't let the old man know or there'll be murders.'

They discussed how to get to Beaconsfield: where was it? – must be a train from somewhere – and how much would it be? Doll would find out and they could go next week. In the middle of all this, three-year-old Pattie was sent to the pie and mash shop with a note and a shopping bag. It wasn't far. Mary, who apparently had no money, paid. Doll said nothing.

Every Friday was the same. There was always something . . .

Robert, somewhere in the desert, doing his National Service, wasn't sending his mother enough money, so Mary had written to his commanding officer. She shows Doll Robert's letter, raging that he had been humiliated and got a bollocking from his superiors, and saying that when he gets home he'll slit her fucking throat. Mary cries, baby Ron cries. Doll soothes one but not the other.

Another week . . .

'Hello, Flo, when did you turn up? What's that on your head?'

'Don't go near her, Doll, she's got nits. Go upstairs and stay there.' Flo shuffles off.

'And I think she's used our Winnie's comb, so I'll have to go through her head tonight now. I'm expecting ructions, but there you are. What can I do?'

Sometimes there would be big news . . .

'Vi's back. She's had the baby, and if you ask me it don't look a bit like Korim Uddin's part of the world.'

'Mum, don't start all that. Has she given it an English name or a darkie one?'

'George, she's going to call him. Well, I hope he behaves a bit better than my one. We'll have to get up to Aldgate to see her, the old man won't have her in the house.'

Sometimes Woodford would be invaded. Mary's timing would depend on her level of desperation. If it was eleven o'clock in the morning, midweek, she had sheets and curtains to sell to Doll's neighbours, in-laws, even Doll herself. If she came at teatime, when Len was there, it was serious. If she sent Flo with a note later than that, it was meant to be very serious:

Hello you two,

I do hope all's well and that I might see you on Friday as per, Doll. Anyway, you know me, and I would only ask you this if I was desperate, and I'm afraid I really am. I've been helping out one of my poor old neighbours with a few bob here and there, doing my best, and she dropped dead yesterday. So I can't get my hands on my owings, and her family are being a bit cagey, to say the least. Anyway, they are up to their eyes with the funeral and what not, so to say I'm embarrassed is not the half of it. One of my tallymen is being a bit off and threatening to take me to court. The old man is going hairless with worry. If I could just have ten bob to keep him quiet, I'll be able to pay you back as soon as. If I don't pay him in the morning – he's coming with the bailiffs – they'll arrest me there and then, as I don't have anything in the house that's worth taking. Sorry to drop this on you both.

Love,

Mum (Mary) x x x

A court appearance was highly probable, and Doll and Len could visualize Mary doing six months in Holloway, with themselves looking after George, Pattie, and Carol in their two rooms. Win was doing shift work as a bus conductress so she couldn't do it. And what about the old man, how would he cope? So Flo was sent back with another note:

Mum,

Needless to say, your letter has upset Len and his mum, and neither of them are talking to me at the moment. We don't have anything ourselves, so you'll have to wait till the morning. I'll get to the pawnshop as soon as it opens and put my wedding ring in. I'll do my best to make it before the bailiffs.

This has to be the last time, Mum, because Len was being very sarcastic about my wedding ring and all its connotations, and I know he's not going to put up with much more of this.

Doll.

The next morning would see both of them shushing the kids and waiting quietly for the knock on the door. When it came, Mary would make them wait and wait. Eventually, she'd face the bailiffs with a barrage of poverty and heartbreak. They would go away with half of what Doll had given her and Mary would pocket the rest.

After a few years, Doll pretended that her wedding ring had become an unredeemed pledge. She never wore it when Mary was around.

Doll saved up and got herself a telephone. She didn't know anyone else with one, so she never really had a bill to speak of, but it did mean that her sisters could call when they needed her. She also hoped it would stop the letters from Mary.

'Doll, can you get over here? It's Winnie.' Mary sounded in a right state.

'Winnie? Why, what's happened? She all right?' asked Doll.

'I can't tell you over this thing. Bring some clobber, you might have to stay the night.'

The phone went dead. It was seven o'clock in the evening. Len and Ron had been fed and were both dozing. Doll bagged a few things together, picked up Ron, and stirred Len.

'Sorry, darling, something's happened at the old lady's. It's my Win. I'll be back tomorrow.'

Before Len knew what was happening, she was off.

Win was lying on the bed, white as a sheet and sweating. Thick black blood dripped down her legs, her face was swollen, and a black eye starting to show itself.

Mary was doing her best with towels and hot salted water. They heard Bob come in from the pub. Doll flew down the stairs to greet him.

'You fucking stupid wicked old bastard. If she dies, I'll have you up there on a murder charge, you bet my life. And you wouldn't be the first in your poxy family, would you? I know all about that, don't you worry.'

Bob coughed some phlegm into the fire, collapsed into his chair, hung his head in shame, and wept. She looked at him, left him to himself, and went back upstairs.

Win was pregnant – or maybe not, now. The previous night, Bob had been told that his twenty-year-old, unmarried daughter was up the duff. You couldn't say he took it well. It helped that Win wasn't at home at the time. He went to the pub. By the time he got back, Win was tucked up in bed. He was drunk. Mary kept her fingers crossed that he'd either forgotten about it in his stupor or would just fall asleep. But it wasn't going to be that kind of a night. All because of Mary's answer:

'She said she don't know.'

Mary was doing her Stan Laurel. She did the best she could under the circumstances. She thought it sounded better than 'No, she can't get married, the bloke's already married with a five-year-old son.' But it was the 'She don't know who the father is' that sent Bob on the befuddled rampage. He dragged Win out of her bed and punched her and punched her. Around her head, in her stomach, all over her, until both fell exhausted. To be fair to Mary, she tried to pull him off. So did five-year-old

George and nine-year-old Carol. Flo and Pattie disappeared into the ether.

Win couldn't go to work the next day because of the state of her face, and she couldn't walk properly. The cramps and bleeding had started late that afternoon.

Doll and Mary sat up all night with her. They put a hot-water bottle on her belly, gave her some aspirins that she didn't want to take, mopped up the blood, and put cold rags on her face. Doll said that in the morning she was going to get the doctor.

Amazingly, Win recovered enough to go back to work the following week. More amazingly, she was still pregnant. Her Dad had knocked one out, but she had kept one in. She would have had twins.

Seven months later, Doll became a godmother to Roberta Alexandra Mary.

'Sounds like the name of a fucking ship,' said Vi.

Bob thought he'd been forgiven, that the Roberta bit was named after him and the Mary bit after his wife, and that the Alexandra bit was Win being regal.

But Doll knew, Vi knew, and, of course, Mary knew – even Carol knew – that Roberta was named after her father, Robert Alexander. The Mary tag was to keep Mum quiet and Dad off the scent.

Doll had wanted her to be called Cherry. She wasn't sure she should be named after a father she would probably never know. There was something unlucky about it.

Cherry was a name none of the sisters could come to terms with, and they teased her about it.

'When you got Ron, you called him Ron, not Farquhar or Winston, didn't you? Cherry, my arse.'

So Roberta Alexandra Mary it was to be.

★

When Ron was coming up for five and about to start school, Doll thought about getting herself a part-time job. Maybe she could save up and buy Len a car. She was restless, not sleeping well. She thought of when she had slept with her mother as a child and the night terrors that Mary would suffer. She had always put that down to her mother's guilty conscience. So why wasn't she sleeping? She had nothing to feel guilty about.

She woke up to the sound of a dog whelping – it was coming from her. She was shaking and sweating. Len held on to her and tried to calm her. She had to get up and have some water, and no, she didn't want him to get it. She turned on the light – and didn't notice for a long while. It must have been a good ten minutes before she saw, and then the breath went out of her.

The Chinaman's teeth.

They were gone.

After they had got over the shock, she and Len searched high and low for those teeth. Teeth that hadn't budged for Mary's pliers over twenty-five years before. They asked each other, could they have been missing for some time and they just hadn't noticed? No, because Doll loved her regular polish of him, he was the only decent ornament she had. She thought of Uncle William. She thought of ghosts. She decided – and she knew it was silly – that Uncle William was trying to tell her something from beyond the grave.

Her period didn't come.

She told her mum and sisters about the Chinaman and his missing teeth. Nobody laughed.

'They're ivory, those teeth. You sure Mrs Harris hasn't had them?'

'Well, you couldn't get them out even with pliers, Mum, could you? Remember?' Flo piped up, which made the others hoot.

Doll told them how when she was small Mary would have nightmares about him coming into the room.

'Yeah, you're all laughing now, but you just wait and see – it's fucking cursed, that thing is. Why don't you just get rid of it? It must be worth a few bob.'

Doll's period didn't come for a second month.

She moved the Chinaman into the front room, rattled his head in case he'd swallowed his ivories, kissed him, and waited for Len to come home.

'I don't know how we've done it, but we have. I'm pregnant.'

Thirty years old, Doll was over the moon, and so were her sisters. She had no idea that one of those sisters was even more pregnant than she was. Neither had Mary or Bob.

When she got to her mum's on the Friday, it was mayhem, the school holidays.

There were Carol, George, Pattie, and little Roberta, ranging in age from eleven down to eighteen months. Then there was Vi with her three-year-old George, and Doll herself with five-year-old Ron. Flo was on the missing list again, Win was at work, Bob was at work, and Robert, home from National Service, was also at work. The children played and shouted, and the women hammered out their gossip.

Doll gave Mary a look without Vi noticing. Mary shrugged her shoulders and shook her head. Something was up. They could smell it off each other.

'Everything all right with Korim, Vi?' asked Doll.

'Lovely, ta, he's got himself a little job cabinet-making in Whitechapel. How's your Len doing?'

They went all round the houses: 'Winnie still seeing him, is she?' 'Do you think he'll leave his missus?' 'Pat Jones been round?'

When it got to Mary discussing the whys and wherefores of having Roberta adopted, explaining that Win was not really up to it at the moment, Vi cracked. She got her purse, handed money to Carol, and told her to take all the kids for pie and mash and go to the park afterwards. Doll let Ron go with them, which was unusual, as she saw that Vi had her serious face on.

'Flo's had a baby,' she said.

'What? How do you mean? How?' Mary and Doll chimed together.

'What the fuck are you on about? You know how. And he's as black as the ace of spades an' all,' Vi shouted at them.

They weren't exactly shocked, more perplexed. Trying to work out the last they had heard of Flo – could she have been pregnant then? Had she looked a bit pregnant?

'What sort of black? Are we talking Joe Louis or your Korim kind of black?' Mary was fuming now.

'Where is she?' asked Doll.

Vi answered all their questions as nimbly as she could: it was a baby boy, a week old, and very Indian.

'He's not your Korim's, is he?'

'Do yourself a favour and shut up, Mother. No, he's not.' Vi gave Mary one her looks.

There was more. Of course there was.

'I'd be ever so grateful if you'd let me get this out in one lump, and not interrupt,' said Vi, lighting a cigarette.

'I'm taking the baby on. Shut up, I told you not to interrupt me, so you don't have to worry about even mentioning it to Dad, okay? No one knew she was pregnant, no doctors, nothing. She just basically had the gutsache for a few hours, pushed, and there he was. The other thing you don't know about is, I'm on bail at the moment – it don't matter what for – but if I've got a tiny baby they probably won't bang me up again. Korim's quite happy about it, he wants to give the kid more of a chance than it would have with Flo dragging it up. Or, more than likely, you'd end up with it, Mum.'

'What about birth certificates and what not?' asked Mary, trying to take all this in.

'It's all been dealt with and paid for. It's all above board now, so don't you worry about it.'

Vi dared either of them to contradict her.

'Oh, blimey,' was all that Doll could manage.

On her way home she contemplated telling Len, but decided to leave it.

Doll gave birth to a beautiful, healthy baby girl. Now she had one of each.

On the first Sunday that she was allowed to travel, arrangements had been made for the whole clan to meet up at Mary's to 'wet the baby's head'. This meant beer down the pub for the men and tea indoors for the women. It was 1950, and Korim and Vi had been accepted after a fashion by Bob. The kids were sent to play on the bombsite opposite the house.

'Barbara. We're calling her Barbara.'

Everybody looked at the baby, looked at each other, sniffed the air, and shook their heads.

'You can't call her Barbara, Doll,' says Vi.

'No, no, no, the last thing she looks like is a Barbara,' Mary states.

'She might grow into it, of course, but she's more of a Cherry, don't you think, Mum?' Win says.

It took years before they would let her forget it.

Getting pregnant had been miraculous and she didn't need to do it again – she had Ron and Barbara, and that was enough. Doll wanted to get on in life, maybe even buy a house one day. She went to the family planning clinic. It made her feel fertile and womanly to have eggs to worry about.

'You do what with it?'

Doll delved into her shopping bag and got out the wrapped contraption.

'Here Vi, come and have a look at all this paraphernalia,' Mary shouted into the scullery.

Doll laid it all out on the kitchen table: diagrams, tubes of lubricant, and a rubber contraceptive cap.

'How do you get the size of that up your clouts? Got a fanny like a horse collar, have you?' Mary sneered.

'What happens if you cough? Will it fall out?' Vi asked.

By the time Doll had explained how it all worked, and that you had to practise inserting it in front of the nurse in case you put it in inside out, they were beside themselves.

'You have to lubricate that side there, then crouch down as if you're having a wee, bend it like this, hope you've done it the right way up, and then this happens.' It flew out of Doll's hand, across the room, and landed inside the coal scuttle.

'That's what happened to me in the clinic. I couldn't stop laughing and the nurse got the right hump with me. "Go home and practise, practise, practise, Mrs Harris."'

'Be no good for our Flo, would it?' said Mary.

'Not unless you could stitch it to her bits permanently,' Vi offered.

Doll looked forward to her weekends in the tent. She had learned to swim, discovered the dribbling bliss of garlic and prawns, and for most of the year sported a tan. Everyone else had a prison pallor.

When Barbara started school, she found herself a part-time job as a chambermaid in a cheap hotel, then as a helper in an old people's home, calling herself a nurse even though she wasn't. She was funny, naughty, daring, and had the ability to breathe the love of life into almost anyone who wasn't yet buried. She worked and she saved, saved like a demon. No one was ever going to take her back to the lino and lavatory life.

Which was just as well. The house in Woodford was going to

be repossessed by the landlord and sold off. He kept to the letter of the law and gave his long-term tenants, Mr and Mrs Harris, first refusal, at a discount. But the old Harrises couldn't see how at their age they would ever be able to manage that much debt, and they didn't have the imagination to discuss it with Len and Doll. For six months they lived in the hope that the landlord would have a change of heart. Doll came in from work and found the pair of them sitting in their coats, crying. She was shown the repossession order. They all had one month to find somewhere else to live.

Doll walked round her little garden and thought of the fifteen years she had spent turning it into Eden, as she waited for Len to come home.

She took the next two days off work and badgered the local council for help, which was a complete waste of time. Mr and Mrs Harris had decided to move in with their daughter a few miles away, so they were going to be all right. There was nowhere for Doll, Len, and the two children to park themselves, though.

After work Doll would walk the streets, trying to find somewhere decent to live. Two weeks later she found a house with a manageable rent, and decided that if they took it for a year, at the end of it they might have saved enough for a deposit to buy their own.

Late afternoon, and Doll had one week left in Woodford. A knock came at the door. Doll was up to her eyes, packing up, clearing out, trying to keep the kids occupied. Her in-laws had already moved out.

Another knock at the door. She recognized what he was by his suit.

He was asking for his money. Three thousand pounds. She laughed and told him he must be at the wrong address.

No, there it was, the paperwork, her name, her signature – for towels, sheets, blankets, hundreds of them.

'You're opening a hotel, I understand.'

It finally dawned on her.

Mum.

'I bet you'll understand this,' she said, tearing up the paperwork and tossing it over his shoulders. 'That was never my signature and I'll have you and my fucking lovely mother up for fraud if you don't piss off away from my doorstep.'

She shut the door in his face and stood trembling with more aggravation than her body and brain could stand. She couldn't do any more packing and just paced the flat, brooding, waiting for Len to come home. He didn't know what hit him.

'Don't take your coat off, we're off to the old lady's.'

And Mary didn't know what hit her.

Her children had been trained since birth never to mention their mother's doings in front of Bob. Doll was well past caring about all that now. The shouting and hollering was interspersed with Len saying, 'Calm down, Dolly.' Bob was asking, 'What hotel? What are you on about?' Mary shouting, 'It wasn't me. Why are you pinning this on me?' The kids were crying, Doll was crying. Mary was looking old and attempting to cry.

Len took Bob to the pub and left them to sort it out. In the end Mary owned up and said she thought that Doll would have moved out by the time the tallyman came for his money.

'Where's all the stuff? What have you done with it?' she shouted at Mary.

'I've pawned it.'

'Well, fucking unpawn it and give it him back.'

'It don't work like that, Doll, he wouldn't take it back. Anyway, I've already sold on the pawn ticket to someone else.'

All the energy left the room. Barbara and Ron sat on two wooden chairs, waiting silently, as if for an execution.

Doll felt her life come full circle: she would never be free of all this scum and detritus she had worked so hard to scrape off.

Mary was disappointed but unperturbed; she had a plan, and it worked. Nobody paid.

The judge looked at Mary Roberts standing in his court and felt a tide of compassion and admiration for this poor, hard-working, hard-done-by scrap of grandmotherhood. To be paid back at half a crown a week, could she manage that? he asked.

'I'll do my best.' she said shyly.

The tallyman lost his job. It would take years before three thousand pounds could be paid off at that rate. She'd probably be dead before then.

Boxing Day 1956

'*A*nd it came to pass afterward, that he loved a woman in the valley of Sorek, whose name was Delilah.

And the lord of the Philistines came up unto her, and said unto her, "Entice him, and see wherein his great strength lieth, and by what means we may prevail against him, that we may bind him to afflict him: and we will give thee every one of us eleven hundred pieces of silver."

And Delilah said to Samson . . .'

I hadn't heard this bit before. I liked the story of Noah best because Granddad would drift off into telling me about the ocean and India – India, where they had chained ladies in cages who were for sale for one night, then apparently you had to give them back to their owner . . .

I asked if this was the same as the story about the lady who had a head on a plate, and Granddad said, 'No, you've got muddled up, she was another piece of work, called Salome.'

I thought about Delilah and her pieces of silver. I thought about the Indian ladies for sale. I thought about the man's head on a plate, like a Sunday roast.

'Is everybody for sale, Granddad?'

'Only those that want to be.' I waited for his teeth to drop down but they weren't there.

In the corner, Uncle Korim was still asleep sitting up, mumbling gentle salaams, his head nodding invisible greetings.

I can't remember when I first learned the 'salaam alaikum', and the return 'alaikum salaam', but we all knew it, we all said it. No, that's not quite true – Granddad never said it.

I'd interrupted his flow but I could tell that he had had enough of struggling with the small print in the Bible, his Bible that smelt of old walnuts. Before I put it back in the drawer, I sneaked a look at the handwritten name inside. I'd seen it thousands of times, but I needed to mull over all the other bits and bobs I'd collected today.

Ernest Bauckham.

'What do you want to be when you grow up, Rob? Given it any thought? See, I knew I wanted to go on the ships from as far back as I could remember. Since the war it's been all right for a girl to want to be something, so what do you reckon?'

I climbed back onto his lap and it dawned on me that I had never asked myself this question. I thought being grown up was about what you looked like, who you might get to run errands for you. But as I never got that many moments to chat to Granddad on my own, I thought hard about it.

'I want to be . . . clever,' I said.

'Clever with what? For what? Clever can make you miserable. Haven't you heard that ignorance is bliss?'

I had heard it mentioned. Mum would say it when speaking about someone she didn't like or was disapproving of. The aunts would say it about Aunt Flo. They had said it today about the Galoot and Carol's eye.

'You, as a young lady – and you will be before too long – have been put on this earth to become what is called "an agreeable rut of life".' He looked at me in a depressed way, as if he had said something wrong.

I had no idea what he was on about.

'Don't become an "agreeable rut", Rob. Make sure you're a bloody disagreeable rut. Then you'll stand a chance.'

'I just want to be clever. I want to know who worked out you could eat mushrooms and not die? Who invented bricks? How did the Eskimos know that if you built a fire in your igloo it wouldn't melt? Why do we speak English and other people French and Chinese? Who invented letters? Where do stars come from? Who worked out that two and two make four? How do you know when an egg is an egg and another egg is a chick? And hanging, what's that all about?'

Of course, there were loads more questions, but these were the ones that had cropped up today.

'You're a queer hawk, you are,' he said, and ruffled my fringe.

Buster started to stretch in the armchair opposite and Uncle Korim sat up with a start and smacked his lips.

'He that hath knowledge spareth his words ...' Grandad whispered.

From the double action of his lips moving and his hoiking his body out of his chair, I worked out that I had been talking too much. Off he went to the lavatory, undoing his belt as he was going. The elsewhere din of the house drowned out 'He that hath knowledge ...' – the cousins pounding the ceiling above, Uncle Korim clearing his throat, his eyes now open.

CHAPTER NINE

Vi

Seven years old and real silver and pennies in her pocket: it was irresistible. Her mum would be champing at the bit, in need of the speedy return of that cash. She knew she'd get a wallop, but it was her wages for all that traipsing around in the cold and wet, selling on her mother's half-stolen linens. That's the way Vi saw it, anyway. Off she'd go, never quite getting lost enough, buying cakes, comics, cigarettes – daring herself, pushing herself into the land of the fearless.

In the end she got what she wanted. She wasn't allowed to run these errands any more. It dawned on Mary that she couldn't trust her. Vi discovered another kind of freedom for herself: she knew she had to get on that bus and see where it would go. Vi wanted some fun. Stealing a bottle of milk is fun. A packet of cigarettes is fun. Getting caught is not.

Vi's timing would get better as she got older, but this night she blew it. She arrived home at exactly the same time as a slightly pie-eyed Bob. It was so dark that she almost knocked him over on the front step. For one tiny second, Vi thought he was some murderer waiting to do her in. Bob knew exactly who she was. He could feel the cheap perfume slurring his senses. Vi was flushed with a mix of fear and pleasure, peroxide blonde waves framed her tiny, sharp face, her lips encrusted with dried-up bright red lipstick. Fourteen years old. Her old, knee-length brown furry coat with its three ginger buttons hid the saucy red frock underneath. The only give-away to her tart's promise was the paste brooch pinned to her coat collar. If Bob had seen the frock, with its low, heart-shaped neckline and ruching up the side of one leg, he would have slaughtered her. He almost did.

Vi's lovely green eyes were smudged with black. She had on well-worn high heels, and the coat that had once been some kind of animal. There she was, standing in front of Mary.

'It suits you,' she said, carefully surveying Mary's near bald head and swollen black eye. 'He should have made that a pair, then at least it might look like make-up.'

'How did you get in? When did you get in?' Mary said, as she pushed Vi's hands away from her sore face.

'I never left, did I? I just slammed the front door and hid behind the coats on the rack till he went off to bed. Then I crept upstairs and slept in Doll's bed in case he woke up and started again. He wouldn't go into her room, would he? Anyway, let me tell you about this bloke.'

Vi should have had a good war, but it nearly broke her.

In crusty working boots and heavy dungarees, she still looked a treat. She shone like a beacon signalling trouble, with her bottle-blonde hair, crimson lipstick smudged with soil. Crouching in the freezing cold and wet, aggressively plucking the Brussels sprouts, she wished the Germans would come and take her away from all of this. Fuck the war. If it's that necessary, let Hitler and Churchill punch it out round for round in the ring. Don't drag me into it.

She tried her best to get on with the other girls. They had all been in a little bit of bother with the law, so weren't respectable enough to be in the Land Army. She was in the 'bottom of the pile brigade' and she detested it – detested the countryside, the ugly locals, the quiet. To cap it all, one bus a week. Which went where? To another pointless, closed-all-day kind of place. Please attack us! Attack us! If only the bombers would come, she could pretend to be dead and walk away into a new life.

All dressed up in one of her two frocks, she had pencilled the backs of her legs with a black line to make it look as if she was wearing stockings. Vi hopped onto the bus as if she owned the company. She was exhausted. She had spent the previous evening telling everyone how ill she was. In the night, she crept out of bed, drank as much tap water as her stomach would hold, then stuck her fingers down her throat and threw up. Her sick symphony churned the guts of the beholders. She was allowed to stay in the warm and the doctor would visit her later that afternoon. She had to get a move on. As the trucks had driven away to take the girls to the fields, Vi had dressed, got made up, and gone through the others' belongings, pinching anything that might be worth something.

Not too sure whether Lincolnshire was nearer to France, Scotland, or London, she hoped at least to get to a city. Vi disappeared for about twelve weeks. The police, of course, tried to find her. Their first port of call was her mother's house, but Mary Roberts and her brood were moving addresses every six months so it took some energy on their part – and there was a war on.

When Vi resurfaced, she had developed a slight northern accent. The law would never find her now, anyway she'd only pinched a few quid and she had a different name, Mrs Baker, a married woman.

Stanley Baker was like a film star, in a spivvy, rough-trade kind of way, and she absolutely adored him. He wore an RAF uniform from time to time, but nobody really knew the where, what, and how of him. He could get anyone their 'extras'. To all intents and purposes he and Vi were happy. They lived off the fat of the war in a couple of rooms not a million miles away from Mary.

What nobody saw was Vi's disgrace: the loneliness, the rows, the good hidings. As quickly as Stanley had waltzed into her heart and beat it up a bit he waltzed out.

Vi would never let it happen to her again.

She decided her mother had been right all along.

'You're sitting on a gold mine, don't waste it.'

She disappeared. Not completely this time.

Nobody in their right mind would have wanted to live in Aldgate. It was full of slum housing, noise, shit, robbers, and was in the thick of the bombing. Some people didn't have a choice, though. Vi would make this her kingdom for the next fifty years. In the beginning, she shared a hovel with Jessie, a nifty backstreet abortionist, who would stay her pal for years. The two of them pleated seamlessly into this black-market world, where everyone had a secret. Outside of the outsiders were the Lascars, Indian seamen. White women seen talking to them were called brazen; white women walking along with them, living near or with them, were branded whores. Vi couldn't give a monkey's.

Korim was kind and gentle, a bit older than her, but she liked that. They had seen each other around, went out for a while, went off with other people, then got back together again. They shared their debts and worries, he taught her some Urdu, she taught him her idea of a bit more English. There were no rules; they lived their lives the best they could.

Vi was pregnant. They decided to make a go of it. She warned him that, whatever happened, he was never, ever allowed to criticize her. No matter what she might or might not do.

He didn't visit her in Beaconsfield – she didn't allow him to. The word 'prison' was never mentioned – just 'I'm being detained at His Majesty's pleasure.' She thought this would fox him, but he knew. He knew she had been dealing in knocked-off stuff and had been unlucky. He hoped she'd come back to him.

Because of the pregnancy, she only had to do three months.

Vi would visit Mary and the others when she knew her dad was at work, and Flo would visit her in Aldgate. Vi would show her off and give her quite a good time. Flo was useful to her, running errands, doing housework, being at her beck and call. She was a built-in skivvy.

Apart from the tricks learned at her mother's knee, Vi had gathered quite a few more from the land girls and from her time with Stanley. Although the war was newly over, there was still rationing. Vi had ration books in the names of three people, so she was able to live quite well.

Curry houses were set up in scruffy backrooms, where Vi was taught a few basic delights with a chunk of scrag end of lamb and a bowl of rice. She never lost the taste for pie and mash, but curry would become her everyday grub. When little George was born, she kept him to herself. Korim loved him but was allowed no hand or say in his upbringing. George didn't look like Korim, or anyone else the family knew, and Vi kept her secret. He was a beautiful coffee colour, with frizzy hair, full lips, and a broad nose. Vi recognized the value of white skin among her dark-skinned community, never mind in the wider world beyond. She reared him as white.

Little George was nearly three years old before he clapped eyes on his grandfather. After the beating up of Win, Bob had gone to a quieter place in his head.

'He's gone a bit soft in his old age. Come round when he's in and take a chance.' Vi, Doll, and Mary organized a tea party as an excuse to see how Win was doing. Bob would be outnumbered.

'I'm not scared of him any more. Fuck him. If he starts on me he'll be more than sorry.' Vi would bring Little George, saving Korim for another day.

Bob came home from the pub one Saturday lunchtime and there they were – all his girls, even Flo, enjoying their pie and mash and ignoring him. Korim was brought round the following week. In Bob's zipped-up way, he found he liked his new black son-in-law.

'Vi! Vi!'

Jessie was shouting up from the courtyard. She didn't have time to run upstairs.

'Vi!'

She could see Little George through the iron railings of Vi's balcony, two floors above. He was staring down at her.

'Mum, I think Jessie wants you,' he called through the open door.

'What? What're you hollerin' about?' Vi shouted down to her.

Jessie ran off to her flat without answering and Vi knew something was up. She told George to stay where he was and be a good boy, and she flew down the stairs.

A low mooing was coming from the back room. Vi found Flo like an animal on its last legs. They hauled her up to her feet and tried to walk her around the room. Then she pissed all over the floor. But it wasn't piss and it dawned on Vi and Jessie exactly what was happening. Her waters had broken.

'Why didn't you tell me she was pregnant? Why didn't *she* tell me she was pregnant?' Jessie accused both of them. Vi was about to ask the same thing. She had thought it was the curries that had filled Flo out.

After a couple of hours, three confused people became four as Black Gary was born. Flo fell asleep, the baby yelled, Jessie and Vi laughed.

'I'll go and see to my George and wait till Korim gets home, then I'll be back. Don't let anyone come in, don't say anything to anyone. Give me a couple of hours to get this sorted.'

She left Jessie half a packet of fags and ran back home. George was still doing what he had been doing when she left him – nothing – just staring out through the bars of the balcony. She gave him a slice of bread and jam, a glass of heavily sugared cold tea, and pondered the afternoon's happenings.

She fancied this little baby. A complicated story simplified itself.

The Uddins crossed the water to South London where nobody knew them. It went like clockwork.

The doctor couldn't have believed the cock-and-bull story that she had given birth on a merchant ship while sailing from India to visit her family here in London. Yes, she would like to be examined even though she felt perfectly all right, but her husband wouldn't allow it because of his religion. Could he check out the baby and give her the bits and bobs she needed to register him? Korim kept up a rumble of Urdu to add to the performance. Weighing up the pros and cons, the doctor relented. The baby looked like Korim, looked fit and healthy, and the mother appeared well and strong. He signed what he had to and got rid of them. Lying was a habit Vi never got out of. The war gave her many gifts, bombed-out houses, lost birth certificates, new papers, new names.

Baby Gary, born to Flo (sister number one), was passed over to Vi (sister number three), and named on his birth certificate as Win's (sister number four). Win was never told.

Vi did her best to love Gary as much as she did George, but he would remain a foreigner to her. George was saucy, lively and unpredictable. Gary was slow, like his mother, and very black. George was ashamed of having a black brother. 'He's not my real brother, my mum felt sorry for him and bought him.' That's what George would say, and that's what Gary would hear. As with Flo, these things would sting in the moment and then float off into the ether. Gary didn't have a mind that knew how to dwell anywhere for very long. Vi was a goodish mother in her ramshackle way. She had been brought up like this and it hadn't done her any harm. Gary ended up belonging nowhere. His sister, the very white Pattie, didn't belong anywhere either.

Over the years Vi learnt enough Urdu to get by. Her prime need was to know what others might be saying about her. She put it to good use, helping the illiterate in whatever tongue with housing forms, visits to the doctor, writing letters. She became Queen White Woman of her patch. Every Christmas was spent at Mum and Dad's. Most of the others would be there with their various kids, and all of them loved Korim. While Mary and her daughters gossiped, argued, prepared the dinner, the men would take him down the pub and be very protective of him in their funny old way.

'Oi, come on, you black bastard, it's your round.'

Korim wasn't offended by this term of endearment. Vi called him it, often. He'd hand over his money to Len or one of the others. The landlord allowed him to sit in the pub but not to buy drinks at the bar. 'No, I'll let him come in, Bob, but hide him. If he behaves himself, I'll turn a blind eye.' Vi and Korim never walked along the street side by side or arm in arm. He would walk three paces behind her. She wasn't ashamed of him, she just didn't want people to give her grief. Most of the time they went out separately.

'Hello, Winnie. Hello, Doris,' Korim said to them as he bent down and reached for something under the sink. His prayer mat. He tapped his finger on his head, meaning he wouldn't be long, and disappeared through a curtain into the bedroom. Vi added some tap water to her huge pan of yesterday's curry, took a fag off Win, sat down with her sisters, and gossiped.

'What's the old lady been up to this week?' Depending on Mary's recent tricks, there'd be laughter, tears, or effing and blinding, all against the background noise of Korim's prayers to Allah.

Vi's scullery, with a little gas stove and sink, was in the same room as her sofa, armchair, and kitchen table. Off this room were two small bedrooms, separated by curtains hung in the door frames. The lavatory, with its wooden bench seat, had a real door. Baths were had in the local bathhouse. Korim never went: it was against his religion to sit in his own filthy water. Every day he would wash his whole body standing at the sink. Their dilapidated Victorian tenement, four storeys high, with no lift, was one of four identical blocks of identical-sized flats. A grim fortress to repel passing strangers, it was a place where the lost tribes of the world could protect one another and remain safe.

Mary enjoyed her trips to Vi's. It reminded her of Poplar all those years ago; the edge of danger livened her up. Bob rarely went; it depressed him. Win would visit on her way back from Moorfields eye hospital, which was round the corner, when she had to take Buster for his check-ups, and that's when Doll would sometimes tag along.

'Check the lav for me, Doll,' said Win.

'Don't forget this, if you're going in there,' shouted Vi, as Win followed Doll out into the tiny passage.

Doll checked that it was spider-free, and Vi handed over squares of newspaper clipped together with a wooden clothes peg. The three sisters giggled and Win went into the lav for her private moment. The family never got used to Korim wiping his arse with his hand instead of paper.

'He eats his food with his hands as well. It's not very hygienic, Vi, is it? That's how you get typhoid,' said Doll.

'How many more times? He eats with his right hand and wipes with his left. It's a religious thing, stop going on about it. He's not asking you to do it, is he?'

The Roberts family enjoyed swapping salaam alaikums and alaikum salaams with him, but they were very cagey about shaking his hand – they could never quite remember which hand was for what. They mostly hugged him, to be on the safe side.

Korim died and Vi didn't really mind. They'd had a reasonable time together. His younger brother, Fahir, newly arrived from India, had been living with them for the past few months and they got on quite well, so she married him. Vi was pushing forty; he was twenty-eight, a bit of a womanizer, a gambler, and lazy. She had had nearly eight years with him when he dropped dead after coughing a lot. Fahir's brother, or maybe cousin – she never could get to the bottom of it – was thirty-year-old Raj. Vi married him a few weeks after the funeral. The family couldn't keep track of all these foreign names and Vi's husbands were now referred to as Raj, Taj, and Bobtail.

Boxing Day 1956

'*D*o you ever come across him, Win?' Aunt Doll was almost whispering.

They were huddled around the fire, Nanny in her armchair, Aunt Doll opposite, and dining chairs had been moved over for everyone else. They looked like they were at the doctor's.

Mum mumbled something I didn't catch. They all turned round and gawped at me. I put my head down and carried on playing dominoes with Ron, Pattie, and Barbara. Little George had gone out with Big George, and they had been ordered to take Black Gary with them. That was hours ago. It was getting dark outside.

I caught a few 'mmm's and then '. . . arrangements to see her or anything?' I felt another turn to look at me, but I was studying the dominoes. '. . . bet she's giving him a dog's life . . .'

'Hurry up Rob, it's your turn.' Ron nudged me.

'He was holding out his hand for my fare, and I said, "I'm Flo, her sister, don't you remember?"' Aunt Flo had forgotten to hush her voice.

'How could he ever forget you, after what you did?' Mum said. She sounded really ratty.

'Come on, Winnie, we don't need to go over all that again,' Nanny said.

'Rob, go and put the kettle on and make us a lovely pot of tea. Ron, Barbara, you go and help her. Go on. And Pattie, the coal bucket's a bit sparse.' Aunt Doll always tried to make everything feel like a game and I knew they wanted us out of the way. Ron and I trooped off, dragging our shoulders to make ourselves look pathetic and making long moaning noises. Barbara copied us and we ran down the passage laughing.

CHAPTER TEN

Win

'*H*ow many more times? You're too late,' said Win.

The old boy stared at his scrap of paper, gave Win a 'fuck you' look and tore it up. He tossed the bits onto the betting shop floor to join the confetti of lost money.

'They're off!'

The shop tannoy screamed the excitement – or not, depending on your horse. Men flocked in from the pub opposite to listen. The door was wedged open with bodies. Win could see the bus stopping outside. It was his. He waved to her from his platform; she pulled a face and waved back.

'I've had a life of regret,' he had said to her the previous week, when she'd jumped on his bus to take the four stops to work. She couldn't get it out of her mind. Was it supposed to make her feel better or worse? She felt both at the same time. That was the problem.

The long gone eighteen years since their last canoodle hadn't taken the shine off Win. At thirty-seven she still had glossy black hair, deep brown eyes, and white skin. She was as skinny as ever. With her wide, straight back, and no chest to speak of, she could have looked elegant if it were not for the size of her feet, which made her walk slightly mannish.

It was 1964.

Robert Alexander Archer. The strawberry blond hair that had shot out of his head as a malnourished thirty-year-old now had the salt-and-pepper speckle of the forty-eight-year-old. His sensual punched green eyes of 'then' had grown into the hooded tamed stare of 'now'.

Win was going to die, she knew it. TB, they had said. Ten-year-old Win looked at the surrounding huts. It did seem a bit nicer than the last place. She'd only been home three weeks from that horrible sanatorium, and now her mum had sent her to this country place.

Win had been prodded this way and that in the sanatorium. She had spent a long month there, and Mary had visited just once. Bob never came. She thought they were going to keep her there for ever, or put her down like a dog.

That was the beginning of her bags of nerveness. Quick movements spotted out of the corner of her eye or loud bangs – any kind of suddenness – would make her jump out of her skin and shake. She didn't grow out of it, and she didn't die in the sanatorium. It wasn't all over quite yet, though.

'She's very pale and underweight for her age, Mrs Roberts,' the young doctor said.

'I know, I know. But I can't get her to eat, doctor. She's tired all the time, cries through the night and what have you. I'm doing my best, but it's obviously not enough.' Mary gave Win a harrowed gaze and sighed. Win looked out of the window. This was the same tale that Mary had told the doctors at the other place. 'Why don't she want me home? I do eat, I'm always starving. She knows Vi pinches off my plate,' Win thought.

'You see, I've got another little one at home, he's eighteen months younger than her, only eight and a half, I'm so frightened about him as well. What if he gets it?' Mary waffled on.

The doctor wrote a version of *War and Peace* into his file and thought it was for the best if Win stayed at least three months –

it would fatten her up, give her plenty of exercise and fresh air, and put some colour in her cheeks.

'You must stop worrying, Mother, you've been told and told she doesn't have tuberculosis. She's just a little undernourished.'

Little Win knew that 'tubercu . . .' meant the same as TB. She stopped looking out of the window and stared at her mother. Mary winked and gave Win a cuddle of a glance.

'Thank you so much, doctor, that's such a weight off my mind. Shall I leave her with you and bring some things for her later?'

Win stayed. She was taken to the clinic block, checked for nits, scrubbed in a bath, and given her Fyfields uniform.

Navy blue knickers.

Navy blue vest.

Grey woollen socks.

Grey woollen pinafore dress.

Grey cardigan.

One towel.

One toothbrush.

These would be washed and changed once a week.

She had never had a toothbrush before. Her mother used to scrub her teeth and gums with a lump of coal a couple of times a week.

Fyfields Farm was ten miles away from the East End in Ongar, deepest Essex, and all the kids came from the slums of London to convalesce after accidents, illness, or plain starvation. They were housed in five long, narrow prefabricated huts. Each hut had a wooden floor, twelve hard single beds, each with a small bedside locker, overhead strip lighting, and smelt of carbolic. Little Win was taken to hut number three by a bandy girl of about thirteen. The girl pointed out Win's place and left.

Win sat stiffly on her designated bed and waited for the supper bell. It was a long time coming.

Eventually the bandy girl came back and took her to the noisy dinner hall. Hot milk and sardines on toast. She would have been able to taste it if she hadn't been riddled with nerves and shyness.

Every morning at six-thirty sharp, the children would have to dress and march through the woods to the bathhouse, clutching a toothbrush, a comb, and the one towel that had to last them all week. The bathhouse was a low brick building with eight mean showers along one side and a row of basins on the opposite wall. At the far end were three cubicles of lavatories. It had a brutal concrete floor and the walls were white-tiled from floor to ceiling. The lavatories gave a speck of privacy with their three-quarter-length wooden doors. Clothes were ripped off, and the scrum for basins, showers or lavs would be survival of the fittest.

Shy, quiet Win didn't have the inbuilt bravado of her mother or her sisters. They would have been at the front, pushing and shoving, first in line for everything. Win was more like her dad, watchful and wary.

Win's skin didn't come to her bespoke. It was off the peg, and it never quite fitted. She wanted to be back home with the others, with her little brother Robert, selling sheets, running errands, being hit by Vi, cuddled by Doll. Anywhere but here with these cocky, lippy kids. After the first two horrible days she spotted someone smaller and more scared than she was. She settled down and wasn't the last one in the shower any more. And she wrote a poem a day, in rhyme.

Win created her own quiet way to manage this new regime, and looked forward to the occasional letter. In the six weeks that she was there she received three: two from Doll and one from her mum. Doll and her boyfriend, Len, visited twice. Mary came only to deliver her and to take her away again. Win kept the toothbrush.

The doctor had been right. Win didn't have TB. Had never had TB.

She was thankful to be back with Robert, the dog, the 'air pie and a run round the table' for dinner. Win would rather be hungry than go back to Fyfields. 'All that marching, marching everywhere,' she'd tell Robert.

They moved house, they moved schools, and, wherever they ended up, Win had that toothbrush. She slept with it under her pillow to make sure that no one else could use it.

Bent and bald, the toothbrush had to be put in the dustbin four years later. Doll bought her another one.

Woodford.

12 July 1940

Dear Win,

I hope you and Robert are behaving yourselves down there and not giving us Londoners a bad name. I know it must have been a bit embarrassing when you were put in the boys' section of the choir, but it's probably because you are more grown-up than some of the others, so don't worry about it. Just keep hollering them hymns; if your voice is that deep, the Devil might be too frightened to pop his head out of his basement. We missed you at the wedding, of course we did, but the two of you are in a much safer place right at the moment.

Mind you, if Hitler does eventually get here, he might reach Cornwall before he gets to us. Only joking. Depends where he's coming from, doesn't it?

I know it's hard not living in the same house as Robert, but you do see him every day at school, and at Sunday school. It's hard for people to take in two kids, and they would always prefer a boy than a girl, especially of your age, so don't take it personally. You could fall in love and what not, and then where would they be?

Anyway, some bad news this end, I'm afraid. It's Uncle William. He's dead. Sorry about this, but he just keeled over and that was that. He didn't suffer or anything, and the funeral is in a few days so it will probably be all done and dusted by the time you receive this. Now, I know you thought the world of him, Win, as we all did. Dad and Granny Clara are really cut up about it. So we need you to be grown up and think of all the nice things. I've written to Robert as well and told him to be nice and caring to you, and if he's not, you let me know and I'll have his guts for garters. You should tell the old maid you're living with about all this, she seems kind. Are you still frightened of her mother? She sounds a wicked old cow. Christians, eh? Who'd have them.

It's been all go here, as you can imagine. It had to be our Flo who found Uncle William, didn't it? She went into one of her turns and got quite mad. She said she found loads of money in the sideboard or something and took it to Mum's. Well, the old lady is denying everything, as per usual. She's had something, though, I know she has. The Chinaman now lives with me and Len. Mum thinks he's got pound notes inside him, an all. The Chinaman that is, not Len. If only.

Did I tell you she took the back off my wardrobe? She's a wicked old cow.

Well, my darling, you take care of yourself, and let's hope this war don't last too long. Len's in the Home Guard, so he won't be sent away. Aren't I the lucky one?

Come back safe and clever,

Your ever-loving sister,

Doll.

Win was given her letter after she had cleared and washed the breakfast things, which meant she was now allowed to open it. But Win wanted to read it alone, not with Mrs Ballard watching her and then asking nosy questions. She asked to be excused, to use the lavatory. It was given suspiciously. Win put her coat on and went to the privy at the end of the narrow garden. It was always cold down there, even in summer. She checked carefully for any insect life loitering and sat down on the pan. 'My letter from Doll,' she thought. She kissed the envelope and ripped it open, and read it. And read it again. Thirteen-year-old Win stared at the letter, which didn't look like a letter any more. She decided to go through each word slowly. Her eyes following her index finger, pointing the way on the pages. Some god had turned a handle on her heart which pumped great globules of tears to run down her face and pushed out a weird, low noise from between her tight lips.

Win and Robert had been six months in Penzance. Mary had put them on the train in London and left them to it. With bread and sugar sandwiches, a label with their name and a gas mask each, they scrunched up together for the long journey to somewhere. The train was filled with hundreds of questions from hundreds of kids – 'What kind of family will we get?' 'Hope they're not old.' 'Hope they're not mad.' 'Bet they'll be posh.' 'They can't separate brothers and sisters, my mum said.'

Robert went to one family, and Win went to Mrs Ballard and her daughter Betty. Mrs Ballard had never wanted to take anyone, but she had been forced to. She had a daughter which meant another girl could share with her. Mrs Ballard was chapel-mean, shrivelled, and sixty. Widowed for twenty years, she still wore black as a mark of her suffering. The few local godless said that Mr Ballard had decided not to wake up one day just to get away from her. Betty Ballard was a fleshy-faced, big-boned young woman of twenty-four with mousy hair. And lonely.

'Winnie? Winnie, are you all right?' It was Betty. Sent to find out what was going on. Win had been in the lavatory longer than was deemed necessary. Betty heard her pull the chain, and then Win opened the door. She didn't look at Betty, she didn't speak, just slowly walked down the garden towards the house. Her left arm was across her chest, reaching her right arm, which she was tapping rhythmically. Betty managed to stop her before she reached the back door.

'Was it your letter? What's happened?'

'I flushed it down the lavatory,' Win said flatly, 'So it's alright now.'

Betty stared at Win's face. It was pinched and tight-lipped, but dry-eyed. There was some snot on her cheek and on her coat lapel, where she had wiped herself into calmness.

'Winnie, please, please tell me about the letter.'

'The Chinaman's gone to live with my sister Doll and she said I'm not to mind about singing boys' parts in the choir,' Win said.

Mrs Ballard was at the back door, thinking sins had occurred in her garden. She tapped her walking stick on the back wall, commanding attention. Betty tried to indicate to her mother that something was wrong, by waving her hand and then putting her finger to her lips. It didn't work. As Win reached the back door, the walking stick was swiped across the back of her bare legs. Betty cried out and Win kept on walking, as if she hadn't felt a thing. She carried on through the house and out of the front door, with tortured Mrs Ballard calling on the Lord for help. Win trudged up the lane to Robert's house, ignoring the mayhem she had left behind her.

Robert wasn't in. She found him playing football in the churchyard with three other boys. Because he was now nearly eleven, he didn't rush up and kiss her like he used to. They stared at each other. Win went and sat on Theodore Quartermaine's gravestone and waited for Robert to come to her.

'I didn't get no letter, maybe it's coming tomorrow,' he said. Win nodded and looked at her sock, which had slipped under her heel.

'Your sock's gone to sleep.'

'So has Uncle William,' Win whispered.

She recited Doll's letter by heart. She could hear her big

sister's voice telling it to her. Little Robert cried. She wiped his tears with her coat lapel and walked him back to his house.

'Behave yourself, and I'll see you in chapel in the morning.'

She went back to face the wrath of Mrs Ballard. 'As long as no one is nice to me, I won't cry,' she thought, 'and that's the most important thing.'

She eventually confided in Betty that night, and Betty promised to get her a stamp and some writing paper. It took her a week to write the three letters, which were all put into one envelope addressed to her sister Doll.

Penzance,
Cornwall.

Dear Doll and Len,

Hope you're keeping well, as this is how it leaves me. Robert took the news of Uncle William not very well, but I've looked after him and he's all right now, I think. Betty (the girl I live with, remember?) kindly gave me this stamp so I could write back. I've put two other letters in, one for Nan and the other for Mum and Dad. Could you give them to them, please? Ta very much. I was upset to hear the news, but with the war on and everything I decided it might be for the best. If, as you say, he just went to sleep in his chair. Did he still have his teeth in? He hated people seeing him without them, didn't he? I think I might be a bit self-ish, because what keeps coming back to me about him is how he gave us all sweets and stories and things, apart from Vi. He couldn't stand Vi, could he? Too stealthy, that's what he used to call her. He must have known she pinched things off him and Nanny. I don't like it down here, but I know it's better than London, so mustn't grumble. Old Mrs Ballard hasn't been too bad since she heard my favourite uncle has just died, but how long it will last is anyone's guess.

Love to all, don't forget us down here,

Win.

Penzance,
Cornwall.

Dear Gran,

Hope you are well, as this is how it leaves me.

Robert's very well and we've both gone a different colour with all this sunshine and fresh air. The lady I live with is a wicked old cow, but her daughter Betty is very kind to me, so mustn't grumble.

Sorry about the Uncle William business. Doll told me everything. Hope you're all right now. When I get back to London, if there's a London left, I expect one of your special bread puddings.

From your ever-loving granddaughter,

Win. XXXX

Penzance,
Cornwall.

Dear Mum and Dad,

Doll has told me and Robert about Uncle William and we are quite all right now, so no need to worry about us. Robert's doing all right in his house and made a lot of mates. I have Betty for company, and even though she is much older than me she is very kind. You wouldn't be any good down here, Mum, no one is allowed to swear.

Hope you don't get bombed out.

Love

Win.

In March 1941, Win reached fourteen years of age. Time to leave school and get out to work. Mary needed her and her pay packet back in London.

Win did as she was ordered and came home, leaving Robert behind in Penzance. She came back to a house she'd never seen before – a house no one else would choose to live in, in a street that the Germans wanted to flatten. Even the landlord was too scared to come and collect the rent. Close to the docks, close to the railways, 19 Silver Street shone like a beacon, asking for trouble.

Silver Street had once been part of six streets of houses, thirty houses per street, one terrace behind the other, built for local railway workers thirty years earlier. Win's first glimpse was more of bombed debris than of houses. Eight houses remained standing in Silver Street, and number nineteen had been shored up. Behind them, the scene was the same.

For the next four years, until it was peace in our time, Win lived in a state of perpetual terror. She would go to work wherever her mum sent her, duck the bombing, avoid going dancing with American GIs in case anyone thought she was easy, and, for a treat, see her sister Doll in suburban Woodford. Win hated the thought of dancing. Her feet were too big for snappy little steps and she felt a clot trying to move them to music. She got engaged to a nice boy called Arthur, who was home from the Navy, a brother of someone she had worked with when she was at the ball-bearing factory. It was a letter romance, and it was with a letter that she finished it a year later.

Mary had been opening his letters and taking the money orders he sent Win – money for furniture, a wedding, when his war was over. Money that Mary said she was saving up for the right moment. It came out of the blue, really. Win had asked how much money there was because Arthur was hoping to get some leave soon, and she didn't have anything to show him. After going round the houses for a bit, Mary got fed up and shouted that she'd had to use it to keep them all going and that was that.

'There's a fucking war on, madam, or has that passed you by?

Mary didn't wait for another wardrobe debacle.

Win knew that Arthur's money was gone for ever.

Dear Arthur,

This is a very hard letter to write to you, but I know you will understand in the circumstances. Two very different things have happened. Both awkward to say the least. Our house got hit last week and we lost everything. All the new furniture and what not. I know we're lucky to be alive and all that, so let's be grateful for small mercies. The other thing is, I'm sorry I can't marry you after all. I've met someone else. I'm sure he'll never be a patch on you, Arthur, but there we are.

No matter how many times she wrote the letter it sounded wrong and cruel, but it had to be done. Arthur sent another letter, asking her to change her mind, but Mary kept it and Win never clapped eyes on it.

Silver Street crumbled around them with no one harmed, and the family moved on to Salmen Road, Plaistow. Backing on to Plaistow station, it was two miles away from Silver Street, the docks, and a little bit safer. It had three tiny bedrooms upstairs, two rooms, kitchen and bathroom, downstairs, but the lavatory was still out in the yard. Half of Salmen Road had taken a direct hit from the Luftwaffe a couple of years before, but there were ten houses left with people in them.

After the Arthur business, wounded Win began plotting. In 1945 she was eighteen. She looked at the lives around her for inspiration and found none. Not her mother's life, please. Not sister Flo's, with the plate in her head and a dull husband. Not Vi's, living with the Indians and treated like a prostitute. Maybe Doll's, at a push, if she could find a Len – nice, kind, funny Len.

The trouble with Win was that she had no idea that she was an off-kilter beauty, with white skin, black hair, full mouth, and good teeth. She was tall, broad-shouldered, and slim. She came from a family where beauty wasn't noticed or mentioned; only ugliness was worth having a laugh about, and Win's big, broad feet got their fair share of comments.

'I've got myself another job, Mum. I've had enough of factory work.'

Mary marched into the front room from the scullery. She was holding her latest baby, two-year-old George, by one arm and he was yelling with the pain.

'You've done what?'

Win took the baby and shook him up and down to quieten him.

Mary, receiving no response, asked, 'How much?'

'Half a crown more than I'm getting now,' said Win, immediately regretting it, that extra half-crown was now Mary's.

Win had been pulling the same lever, punching holes in identical iron nuts, for nearly a year. She was breathing madness with the noise, the oil, the speed, and she hardly ever saw daylight.

The uniform was fabulously important; she wasn't too struck on the hat, but it was better than wearing a turban as she had had to do in the factory. A bus conductress, a clippie, out in the not-so-fresh air. She stood on the platform of the number fifteen, taking her all the way from East Ham bus garage the eight miles west to Oxford Street. The West End. She got her first glimpse of rich people, walking and talking just like in the films. She worked different hours every week, called 'early turns' and 'late turns', and met all sorts. She was in her element. The job proved that she was good at mental arithmetic because she had to 'pass an exam and everything'. She was as pleased as Punch with herself.

And then she met *him*.

She wasn't supposed to. No one was 'supposed to'.

There were lots of other back-from-the-war blokes working

in the bus garage. Robert Alexander Archer was different. He was quiet. He observed.

A miserable-looking bastard, the rest of the girls called him. He observed Win. He found her isolation, and she his. He was twenty-nine, eleven years older than her. And that was that really.

They had a secret let-me-kiss-you-please kind of romance. He said best to keep it quiet at work, we don't want people knowing our business, do we? She was invited to dinner at his mother's house – a spotlessly clean, brown-toned house that smelt of furniture polish. It reminded Win of her grandmother's. So this was his family: his chatty, busy-bee mum and quiet behind his paper dad; his two brothers, one a Communist, one a Conservative; and Robert Alexander Archer owning up to once being a Fascist in Oswald Mosley's Blackshirts. Opinions on Churchill, the King, the Church flew across the dinner table so fast that Win wasn't sure what she was supposed to do. So she watched. She watched *him*, with his sarcastic put-downs and expressionless face. The others would laugh; he would wink at Win and give her a smile that broke his face and her heart.

Robert Alexander Archer played the piano – not pub piano, something posh and classical – and she whiffed of love for him.

They walked the long way round, through all the dark backstreets towards her home. He pulled her into the half-remains of a derelict house. A rat screamed out of their way. It was a get-inside-me-and-stay-there-for-ever kind of moment. He said he loved her. He said no one would ever love her like he did. But it wouldn't be a forever, forever.

For the next year her big feet floated on air.

When he was working and Win wasn't, she would find his bus and go for a ride with him. He seemed to like that. When he wasn't working, he slept. At least, that's what he said. Mostly they worked the same shifts as that was the only way for them to see each other. When they finished late, they would walk home, chatting and cuddling and laughing all their thoughts and dreams into some kind of relationship. When they finished early, around lunchtime, they would hop on any bus that would take them somewhere pretty. Bus workers travelled for free. In good weather they would head for St James's or Hyde Park, along with other lovers who had no homes to romance in. They fed the ducks, went boating on the lake, and kissed under the elderly oak trees. In bad weather they went to the early afternoon pictures and got romantic in the back row, just like everybody else.

Win had told Doll all about Robert Alexander and Doll told mother Mary. Mary told Vi.

Bob Roberts was told nothing.

They needed to give this boyfriend the once-over.

Win didn't want to bring him home when her dad was there, farting carelessly and gobbing into the fire. Robert Alexander Archer was cultured, knew long words, and wrote her poetry. It was decided they would meet in Woodford, at Doll's. A return thank-you for the tea at his mum's was the best Win could do. Len went downstairs to his mum and dad's.

They liked him, flirted a bit with him, and left Win to get on with it and enjoy herself.

'No one will ever love you like I do.'

Robert Alexander Archer was going camping with his mates for a week. She rode with him on his bus on the Friday night before his Saturday morning departure and she had been going to tell him then, but she wanted to feel happy so she decided to tell him when he got back.

Her week dragged like a year. She felt dead without him.

His first day back at work was to be the afternoon and evening shift. She was on 'earlies'. Win tallied up her day's takings as quickly as possible so she could see him and talk to him before he disappeared out of the garage. She ran through cul-de-sacs of buses until she reached the stand for the number five. He was sitting on the platform, reading the newspaper.

'You look well. Have lovely weather, did you? It's been hot here, as well,' Win blurted out. He looked so handsome and sun-loved, his stern gaze and tight-shut mouth wobbled her heart. 'I was frightened I was going to miss you today. Did my totting up at top speed, hope my sums are all right.'

His driver was calling him to get a move on. He stood up, rang the bell, gave her a wink, and moved off. As his bus pulled out of the garage, he saw her standing all alone, buses moving around her. She was crying, with her eyes wide open.

At ten-thirty that night he came to her house. He gave it the once-over, as a burglar might: one front door, one downstairs window, one upstairs window. He walked away down the street. He would traipse back to the house three or four times, thinking 'I'll leave it till tomorrow', thinking 'Why don't I just knock at the door and ask her what's up?' Finally, knowing everybody was bound to be in bed, he threw stones up at the top window and hoped for the best. Win and eight-year-old Carol, peered down at him.

Win came to the front door with her black hair tied in white curling rags, wearing an old coat over her knickers and vest.

He was sure she was going to leave him, sure she'd met someone else.

It was worse than that. On the doorstep, in shy whispers, they exchanged their secrets: 'I'm so sorry, I'm pregnant,' from Win; 'I'm married,' from Robert Alexander Archer.

'Oh, Rob, no.'

She tried to shut the door on him and all of it, but he pushed his way in and put his hand over her mouth to keep her quiet. They could hear creaks from upstairs and her dad pissing in the chamberpot. Win crept her married man through the house out into the backyard, sat quietly on the pan of the outside lav, pulled her coat around her, and thought of Penzance and the war and the almost-forgotten Betty. His story came out in a lump which took approximately twenty minutes, then he left. He let himself out of the house.

Win tried to picture this 'home' of his: this wife, eight years older than him and nearly twenty years older than Win. His five-year-old son, who had been born after he was sent to Burma. If it were just the marriage, he would leave he'd told her, but he could not leave the boy.

She stayed out there for hours. Every new thought made her remove a couple of the curling rags from her head. The sun came up, poked its nose into the mess of her life, and it was time for work.

Her bus pulled into the garage at the end of her morning shift. She looked for him, thinking that he might have come in early to see her. He wasn't there. Win trudged the length of the noisy high street, and contemplated going to the pictures to have a think in the darkness.

'I'll have a fag when I get to the corner,' she thought.

He lit it. He *was* there. Not in his uniform.

If Rene had seen him leave the house today, she would have known that he had no intention of going to work. He was dressed for a walk in the country: brown cords, white shirt, and brown lace-up boots. His trousers had the double security of a leather belt and elastic braces.

Win puffed on her fag and looked down at their feet. He stared at the top of her shiny rumpled hair.

He wanted her to speak first, but she just couldn't.

'If you ask me to leave her, I will,' he said.

'No, it's not for me to ask. You'll never hear me ask that.'

Win had gone to bed straight after her tea; she was on an 'early turn' and had to be up at four o'clock in the morning. She was miserable.

The punch in the face hurt so much that it became a kind of anaesthetic for the wallops that followed. She couldn't stand up when he knocked her out of the bed. She was senseless, only the words filtered in.

'I married a trollop, who bred trollops. I'm living in a fucking whorehouse.'

'Bob, leave off, leave her alone ... Bob, leave off, for Christ's sake, you're going to kill her.'

'You don't know whose it is? How many fucking blokes you had? Do you work on the buses or your fucking fanny?'

Bob was hitting Win, Mary was hitting Bob, little Carol and George were yelling and holding on to their father's legs, and then it stopped.

Bob reeled back downstairs.

Mary and the two kids helped Win to get onto the bed. She was hardly breathing. Carol was sent downstairs in the dark to get a cup of water for her. George got comfortable at the foot of the bed, tucked his feet under the blanket, and said 'Wicked old bastard.' It would have made Win laugh, but she wasn't able to move her face. Carol joined George at the foot of the bed and Mary got in beside Win.

Doll couldn't believe the sight. The thick blood oozing down Win's legs, her face so swollen that one eye was completely closed. The bed looked like a slaughterhouse. Carol and George were covered in blood. Mary was mopping the never-ending blood with towels and salt water.

Doll was screaming, with no sound coming from her dad at all. 'You fucking stupid wicked old bastard. If she dies, I'll have you up there on a murder charge ...'

Win could feel the pump of her stomach throbbing for a way

out. 'Well, that's that. If I'm not pregnant any more and I live, end of problem. If I die, I won't be pregnant any more, end of problem,' she thought. It was the end of July 1947. The National Health Service hadn't quite been born, either. Win needed a doctor, and the doctor needed paying. Doll paid him.

Mary went to the bus garage and found the married Mr Archer. The distraught mother gave such a pitiful performance about death and doctors' bills that he parted with all the money in his pocket and gave her his watch, which had belonged to his grandfather, to pawn, and promised more.

Mary didn't keep all this money for herself. She bought some good food to help Win get back on her feet and treated her to her favourite thing in all the world, a tin of Carnation condensed milk. Mary wasn't all bad.

'Aren't you the lucky one? You're still pregnant,' said the doctor.

'I've never been on speaking terms with luck,' Win told him.

She trudged from the surgery in the August heatwave to the graveyard of Trinity Church. She needed to sit down. There she attempted to redesign her future. She would have to leave her lovely job, she couldn't face the shame. She'd start a new life as a pretend widow.

She'd have to work, to keep herself and the baby. Who would look after the baby? If only she could move in with Doll, but Doll didn't have any room. Round and round she went, looking for freedom, but for now there was no escape.

'Fuck the lot of them. I'll have to face it out. It doesn't matter, because in the end, whatever happens, I will never be alone again. I'll have this baby, which will for ever be a piece of him. I will change my world with this baby.

On a perishingly cold 26 February, Win struggled to get her little bastard out of herself. The baby must have taken one eyeful at its future and decided to stay where it was. The downstairs front room, which was normally Bob and Mary's bedroom, had been turned into the maternity ward. A fire had been lit to take off the nose-pinching chill. The curtains stayed closed. It was a Thursday.

In between her birth pangs, Win studied the room like she had never done before: the green gloss walls, to fend off bugs apparently, the brown lino with its faded diamond pattern, the iron fireplace which could hold only a cupful of coal. Above her, a bare lightbulb, with its ginger strip of flypaper encrusted with last summer's flies. There were four broken wireless sets dumped under the window, and on the other side of the room an old sideboard with its two doors taken off. Next to the sideboard were two wooden kitchen chairs, where Mary and the midwife sat with their coats on.

Eventually, at ten o'clock that night, Win's daughter lurched into this world and onto the bed of old coats. The baby was placed in a little cardboard box, like a cat waiting to travel to the vet's, and put in the sideboard.

Bob stayed well away in the back room where dozy Flo made tea and kept the fire going. Her little Pattie was fast asleep upstairs, unaware of what was going on. George and Carol sat in the passage with their coats on and debated the whys and wherefores of where babies actually came from. They decided it definitely had something to do with the midwife's bag.

On Friday, 1 April 1966, the day before her eighteen-year-old daughter, Roberta Alexandra Mary Roberts, was to be married, Win sat at her red Formica-topped kitchen table, smoking and looking out of the window. She hoped that Roberta would be back from the florist's before the two boys, seven-year-old Lionel and nine-year-old Buster, came home from school. It was time to put the record straight.

Three floors up in her 1930s' flat, Win had a fine view of her hideous surroundings. Beyond the bombsite almost below her, were a few broken, yet lived-in houses, the Methodist hall, where her sons had been christened, a grocery shop, the cobbler's, three pubs, and the primary school. She could make out a couple of ships' funnels, some cranes, and a few foreign flags. The Isle of Dogs. Six miles away from where she was born, a different country. Every Islander was related to another in some shape or form; Win had lived there for thirteen years and couldn't have belonged even if she'd tried to.

'Mum, it's me.'

There she was, the bride to be. She was the spit of him – except that she had brown hair and not his strawberry blond, her eyes were muddy brown, not his greeny blue. In some ways, Roberta was a smaller version of her mother, with quieter colouring – average height, slim, big feet. What she had of him was the stern, square face and his hidden, hooded look. She was unreadable until she smiled, just like him. She was sarcastic, just like him. And she had the temper of her grandmother.

Win looked at her nearly grown girl and wanted so much for her.

'What's up, Mum?'

'I'd been hoping you'd be home before the kids get back, I have to tell you something.' Win was very serious in her delivery.

Roberta covered her nerves and got ready for a fight. She was eight weeks pregnant and prayed her mother hadn't caught her out. Win put her index finger to her lips, and her daughter knew a monologue was coming.

'You remember when you had to take your birth certificate to the vicar and it only had my name on it as the parent, and I said just tell him your dad left when you were a baby and you don't know anything more? Well, I thought you'd ask me then, but you didn't. You've never asked me about your real dad. I don't know why, but it suited me that you didn't and that you've always accepted what I've told you, like when you asked why your surname's Roberts and mine and dad's and the boys' is Marney.'

Roberta got up and went to the lavatory. She locked herself in for a good ten minutes. Win lit another fag and waited. With no sound of chain-pulling or water running, the young woman who had gone in came out of the lavatory a little girl again, looking guilty, feeling guilty. She didn't know why.

'Can I carry on?'

Roberta nodded and dreamed out of the window at the ships and the flags. Win told her her love story with all its nooks and crannies – how clever he was, how talented, the love of her life.

'Isn't there anything you want to ask me?' She stared at the back of the daughter's head and waited.

'What are you thinking? Look at me.'

'I sort of knew anyway. Nanny told me something when I was fourteen,' said Roberta, still staring out of the window.

'The wicked old bastard, what's she said to you? Why didn't you tell me? I know you think the world of her, she's got you wrapped round her little finger. Why d'you think I married Dad? It was to get you well away from her clutches.'

Then the fatter story came out, all the betrayals.

'It's April Fool's day today, isn't it?' Roberta said.

Two weeks after the birth, Win got herself an early-morning cleaning job. Mary took her wage packet, all of it, but at least Win got to spend most of her time with the baby. She'd meet up with R.A. at the end of her street once a week, and he would take her to the pictures so they could warm each other in the back row. When she missed him really badly, she would get on his bus with the baby and do his journey with him.

'Sorry, Win, the baby's all right, she's soundo. I've just got to pop next door to old Mrs Flanagan.' And with that Mary was out of the house. Win hadn't even taken her coat off when there was a bossy rat-tat at the door.

'Are you Winifred Roberts?'

Win looked at the two hard-faced women, both aged about forty. One was skinny and artificially blonde, the other was mouse-toned all over.

'For your own sake, we'd better come in, unless you want the whole street to hear.' So far only the blonde had a voice. Before Win had a chance, they were in the house.

'Where is it?'

'I'm sorry, I'm not sure I know what's going on. What's going on?' asked Win.

'Where is it? Where's this baby, then?'

All the pennies dropped at once and Win knew she was looking at R.A.'s wife. The other woman remained a mystery.

The wife looked at the sleeping infant, turned to her pal and said, 'Well, he could never deny that, it's the spit of him. Miserable-looking bastard.'

Then turned to Win. 'So. If I left him, would you take him on? Live with him?'

'Yes,' said Win, quietly.

'Really? Then you're never going to have him. Come on, Kitty, I've seen enough.'

As Win opened the front door for them, she asked who had told them.

'Your mother.'

And they were gone.

Boxing Day 1956

'I'm telling you, Doll, if you could get that thing X-rayed, you can bet your boots it would be stuffed with money. All right, if not money, then jewels or something,' Nanny said.

Everyone was crammed in the front room. Tea for us kids was spread out on a big old sheet in front of the fire: ham sandwiches and Nanny's lovely bread pudding, still warm. Up at the table the grown-ups were querying whether the Chinaman really did have a secret stash somewhere. Uncle Korim said that the Chinamen he had come across were very particular where they put their money, they hid it in all sorts of queer places, and that's why nobody ever bothered to try and rob them, it would take too long.

'What's she supposed to do? Take it along to the hospital, say it's not well and needs an X-ray? She'd end up at St Clement's in a straitjacket.' Aunt Vi was laughing, sitting on Uncle Korim's lap. I could tell from the way Aunt Doll and Uncle Len looked at each other that they thought there might be something in this.

'Mary, it's a bloody old carving. It's not a money box, it's not hollow. When will you get that into your head?' Granddad sounded like he had the hump with her.

'Well, it had more fucking teeth than you ever had,' Nanny shouted at him, and that made us all laugh – even Granddad.

'By rights, it should never have been given to you, Doll. Uncle William always promised it to me,' Mum said.

'Oh, leave off, Win. You were just a kid when he dropped off his perch. How could that thing be given to a kid? He promised it to everyone as far as I can tell,' Nanny told her.

The room juddered with noise. From getting the tea organized to finally squatting down to eat, everyone was at full pitch. The men's voices boomed across the table, asking for the piccalilli or the pickled onions, and the women were shouting back louder and higher about 'trying to have a conversation here . . . lost the use of your limbs, have you?'

Big George was eating his sandwich outside on the basement steps with a girl. They were the only ones not making any noise. The last time I'd peeked through Nanny's net curtains, they were sharing a fag.

Barbara didn't want to sit on the floor with us any more and tried to get onto Uncle Len's lap, where Aunt Doll was. Barbara won, of course, and Aunt Doll went back to sit between Flo and Nanny. I was trying to stop Buster from taking the food out of my mouth, Little George kept going to the table to pinch more onions, Pattie was in and out, making cups of tea and filling up the fire, and Ron punched Black Gary for something I didn't quite catch. Nanny was holding Lionel and they were all shocked when she covered her finger in the horrible yellow piccalilli and put it in his mouth. He scrunched up his little face as it took his breath away, then bawled his eyes out and threw up over Nanny's arm.

'Serves you right. Give him here.' Mum got him back and 'there there'd him. My dad was talking about asphalting and the price of lead, what a nice little earner it could be for him and his mates when they were working on roofs. Uncle Len and Granddad were interested in the price of lead, while Uncle Korim was trying to explain to Nanny something about the sandwiches. He wasn't allowed to eat ham for some reason. Aunt Vi ripped the ham out, put some piccalilli and a couple of pickled onions inside the bread, and gave him that, along with a big chunk of bread pudding. Nobody else took any notice, except Ron and me. We were waiting for his head to blow off, but it didn't. He seemed to enjoy it.

'I don't reckon there's any money in the Chinaman,' piped up Flo. As usual, no one seemed to take a blind bit of notice of her. 'Don't you remember? All Uncle William's money flew out of the drawer in the sideboard. That's where he kept everything.'

Nanny checked whether Granddad was listening to this, but he was occupied in conversation with my dad, asking, 'Do they burn much electricity?' and 'How dear are they?' They were talking about televisions. We already had one, and so did Aunt Doll.

'I was so frightened. I thought it was pigeons flapping all over the place.'

Aunt Doll tipped the wink to my mum and Aunt Vi, and all eyes turned to Flo. Nanny was about to be ambushed.

'Leave it out, Flo, we don't need to be raking over William's ashes now. It's Christmas, for fuck's sake.' Nanny gave a nod towards Granddad and raised one eyebrow at Flo, meaning she should shut her trap.

'Hang on there, Mother, you were the one who brought this up.' Aunt Vi said 'Mother' in a really vicious way.

Nanny put her elbow on the table and rested her head in the palm of her hand, looking bored – or maybe she'd given in.

'Carry on, Flo. What were you trying to say?' Aunt Doll pumped her.

'I just don't want anyone to think that I had it all. I've pondered for years over this. Where did it all go? There were bundles and bundles of fivers. I gave it to you, Mum, didn't I?' This wasn't a question from Flo, more of a reminder.

Nanny stayed looking bored, saying nothing, only every now and again giving Granddad a sly glance. He was still talking tubes and valves with Dad.

'No one ever thought you had it, don't you worry.' When Aunt Doll said that, she, my mum, and Aunt Vi all stared at Nanny.

One by one, they put their hands over their eyes, ears, and mouths: the three wise monkeys.

'Will you lot leave off? We're talking sixteen fucking years ago. I can't remember. What I do remember is buying the lot of you brand-new funeral clobber. Where do you think I found the money for that?' Nanny hissed at them. 'William's leavings are in that poxy Chinaman, mark my words.'

Whenever there was any kind of whispering going on, the room would stop and move in on the whisperer. Nanny looked round and caught me with my hand over Buster's mouth. He was getting on my nerves and I was trying to keep him quiet; if I'd been on my own, I would have walloped him. I thought I was going to be told off, but instead Nanny took him from me – which was odd, because she didn't like Buster much.

'I can't imagine the amount of cash that's lubricated your mitts over the years.' Aunt Vi said this to Nanny, though looking at the others all the while.

CHAPTER ELEVEN

Robert

'Get that little bastard out of here, and someone wipe the snot off her – I'm trying to eat my dinner,' he shouted.

Robert was back from his National Service. Egypt had changed him.

Two-year-old Roberta toddled towards him. She had no idea that he was yelling about her. Win grabbed her just in time, scooped her up in her arms, and made a small soothing noise. They both went upstairs to their bedroom: the middle one, the smallest one.

This unknown Robert was back.

'That's enough. You're back home five minutes and now look what you've done,' Bob said to him.

Robert spooned the last bit of his rabbit stew around his brown enamel plate. He'd come home to nine people living in this tiny house. Nothing had changed, except that the people had got bigger and now there was this extra one.

There was his dad sitting in front of the fire, fiddling with bits of radio, trying to build a radiogram. He was wearing the same old clobber: black worsted trousers, worn to a sheen, kept up by elastic braces, a once white but now greyish-blue collarless shirt with some buttons missing, and brown slippers. His mother, Mary, still wore that old rose-printed wrap-around apron over another floral frock. She was moving from scullery to sitting room and back again, checking that dozy Flo was making a pot of tea and doing the washing up hygienically. Pattie, now eight, was doing most of it.

Robert looked at Carol and George, his two youngest siblings, sitting on the floor, aggravating Bob by hiding his radio parts. Carol was a saucy eleven-year-old now, and turning into an auburn beauty. She had flirty green eyes, good cheekbones, and a greedy rosy mouth. She was skinny like the rest of them, but it suited her. Eight-year-old George was a square version of her, with an atom bomb in his belly, fearless, frightening, and clever.

Robert wondered if these two would use their looks and smartness to better advantage than his elder sisters had done. George would do all right if he didn't end up in prison, and Carol could do very well for herself if she didn't get pregnant. He stopped thinking about his family and went back to his own desires. He'd won his first battle, a room of his own. He didn't give a toss where the others slept, he was paying his keep and needed a room of his own to study and be left alone in. Mary had bowed to his every whim, she needed his pay packet each week. So she and Bob slept in the front room downstairs; the three rooms upstairs had Robert in the back bedroom overlooking the yard, Win and her baby in the small middle one, and Carol and George sharing the front bedroom with Flo and Pattie. Sometimes Carol slept with her mum and dad, and sometimes George would sleep with Win and Roberta.

Robert was slowly prising himself out of Mary's grip, though she couldn't quite feel the whole force of it yet.

National Service had taught him the outskirts of potential new skills. It had taught him he could learn anything if he put his mind to it.

'Next year . . . I'm going to be a plumber. I'll have my own business, the lot.'

Robert hadn't come home to roost but to wipe out his history and start again: working, back at his old job with Lyons Corner Houses, night school, work, night school, exams. The rest of the family hardly saw him, and they were grateful for it. Eventually, he didn't bother to speak at all when he was home. He would shout, but made no conversation.

'Shut up. I can't hear myself think.'

Work, wash, eat, go out. When he was in his bedroom studying, everyone else crept around and argued in whispers.

Robert made sure that Mary didn't get to see his pay packet; he just gave her thirty shillings a week. She knew he had more somewhere but, try as she might, she couldn't find it – well, ninety-nine per cent of the time she couldn't.

'Oh, Win, what's she done with Blackie?' Seven years old and Robert knew something was afoot.

'He'll come back, Robert. Don't cry now, else she'll give us both a good hiding.' Win cuddled him and smoothed his hair, looked into his green-speckled brown eyes and tried to make him feel safe.

Little Robert had hollered and hollered for his dog, but the coal lorry carried on its journey to yet another new place to live.

'He don't know where we're going, how can he come back? Can't we see if he's gone to the old house?'

Win looked at him, through him, through herself, and back to him again, kissed the top of his head for a long time, and he knew that was the end of Blackie.

'Next year' was Robert's survival technique.

'Next year, it'll all be all right because I'll be eight and no one will be able to tell me what to do any more. I'll be at school in the big boys' class and school will tell Mum what's what.'

'Next year when I'm nine, me and Win can run away.'

'Next year when I'm ten . . .'

When it happened, Robert didn't run, he got sent: Robert and

Win were put on a train to Penzance, hundreds and hundreds of miles away in somewhere called Cornwall.

Mary was first in the queue to get rid of these two when war started – she was forty years old and had enough on her plate looking after six-month-old Carol. She had hoped her breeding days were over. Her three eldest girls weren't much help to her, what with Flo still living with old Clara Roberts and courting, and Doll spending most of her time at her future mother-in-law's, all over a stupid wardrobe. And Vi. Where was Vi?

Sixteen years old and on the rampage.

Mary put Robert and Win on the train, kissed them both on the lips; they kissed the baby and, choo-choo, they were off.

Robert had spent all his little life glued to Win, and to be put now in a different house from her unnerved him at first. Then he got on with it and enjoyed himself. He saw her at school and Sunday chapel, so it wasn't that bad.

Robert was placed with Mr and Mrs Lowther, the butcher and his wife. They had a lovely shop with a big flat above it and no kids of their own – and all the meat he could swallow. He couldn't believe his luck.

Mr and Mrs Lowther – he would never call them anything else – were almost comic book too-many-pies roly-polies, with rosy cheeks. They let him have the time of his life, so long as he stopped swearing – that they couldn't abide. He didn't do too badly, saving all his fucks and bollockses for the playground, and sometimes slipping one in while singing hymns. The Lowthers gave him a slightly too big for him bike, with a basket on the front, so that he could help them on Saturday mornings, delivering meat to the lazy, the rich, or the infirm.

'It in't 'alf good where I am, Win, I can pinch you some sausages, if you like.'

'Don't you worry about me, Robert, you just behave yourself. They all think us East Enders are thieves and murderers as it is.'

Win and Robert were dawdling their way home from chapel. They had been in Penzance just over two weeks. He was wearing brand-new trousers and boots; his hair was slicked back, and he had a holiday splurge about him. She was wearing her 'other' frock, while her first frock was in the wash, and her old plimsolls, which had been whitened and now had laces, and had her shiny black hair scraped back into a cruel tight plait. There was no holiday splurge around Win.

'I have to wash myself *all over*, underneath the arches and everything, *every day*. Do they make you do that?'

'Yeah. And I have to share Betty's bath every Saturday night after my tea,' said Win.

'I didn't have any nits. Did you?' Robert said proudly.

'Course we didn't. Mum did us before we came away, didn't she? I think they've got a fucking cheek, as if we'd been dragged up or something. They're so high and mighty down here, they should try having our Vi living in their house.' The thought made them laugh out loud, and the talk turned to home.

'I wonder if they've got tallymen down here, Win. Do you remember all them eiderdowns she got?'

They giggled at the memory of two years before, but it hadn't been funny then. Turning the corner on their way home from school, there it was: their house covered in feathers. A lorry-load of eiderdowns, a ladder and the top bedroom window completely removed. The unknown lorry driver was shoving eiderdowns in to Mary, who was hanging out of the windowless window. Half a dozen local wives were sitting outside their houses, either on their doorsteps or on wooden kitchen chairs, knitting, gossiping, and taking not a blind bit of notice. When the job was finished, indoors was mayhem. The top front bedroom was stuffed from floor to ceiling with huge swollen eiderdowns, and feathers were choking everyone.

'Where did they come from, and where did they go?' asked

Robert, the thought coming to him probably for the first time.

'I think the lorry driver must have pinched them from somewhere. Mum's job was to get rid of them, and they shared the winnings,' said Win.

They carried on in silence, Robert churning thoughts around in his head and Win dreading the long, quiet day before her. She took her time and walked him all the way home to the Lowthers' butcher's shop.

'Ta-ta. Be as good as you can and I'll see you in the morning,' she said and kissed him on the forehead.

Robert suddenly asked her, 'Win, what's a red herring?'

'My life, I think,' she shouted back at him and walked off down the road to Mrs Ballard and Betty.

Robert imagined he would live in Penzance for ever. He never wrote home; Win did that for the pair of them. He didn't miss home; he didn't even miss Win when she was ordered back to London. Not a smudge of pain smeared him. Not even Uncle William's death, which had come right out of the blue. Of course, he had felt a bit sorry for Win when she told him all about it that day in the churchyard, but that was all.

He did come back from Penzance – back to his almost old life, a different house again, of course. He was fatter, fitter, and fourteen. The war was nearly over; his own war with his future was about to begin.

'You're starting work on Monday, with your dad at Lyons Corner Houses. Dad will show you the ropes. Be grateful, because these jobs are hard to come by, all right?' Why ask if it was all right? He knew he didn't have a say in the matter and that it had all been stitched up long before he was back in London. His mother thought choices were only for the feeble-minded.

'You'll like it, travelling all over the place, West End and everything, meeting all sorts, and the pay's quite good.' Mary was telling him all this in the long queue in the pie and eel shop. Robert stared around him, at the sawdust on the floor, the black and white tiles covering every inch of the deep, narrow room, and the six long, marble-topped tables. The benches on either side were full of customers coming and going, pushing along to make room for others. The cook was running from his kitchen laden with a tray of thirty-six hot pies, plonking them down for his wife to dish out as fast as she could to the waiting line, and scooting back into his kingdom for more pies.

'More liquor pretty soon, Charlie boy,' she shouted after him.

An old boy in cap and overcoat at the head of the queue said through his three brownish teeth, 'No, I'm not sitting down, I just want some eels to take out, thanks, darling.'

'Charlie-e-e-e, where's the poxy liquor? Come on, get a shift on.'

It was their turn. Mary ordered – without asking what he wanted, of course. Robert moved to the end of the counter to pick up two forks and two large spoons, and found a space for the two of them on one of the wooden benches. She'd bought him two pies, double mash, and liquor, which he immediately doused in salt and vinegar. This turned the green slimy liquor – a parsley sauce mystery – into a striped deliciousness. Mary had treated herself to a plate of jellied eels.

'You're onto a good thing with this job, boy. Don't fuck it up and you'll be laughing, I'm telling you.'

She had a mouthful of masticated eel and was fishing the bones out with her fingers. He didn't answer, he was too busy eating and thinking – thinking, 'She's got fat, really fat, while I've been evacuated.'

Mary hadn't told anyone yet, because she didn't know herself, that she was pregnant again. She was forty-three years old and seven months gone. When the doctor told her that no, it wasn't wind, but a baby, and she told the family, Mary had just eight weeks to prepare for it. Robert, fresh from evacuation, was about to get a baby brother.

He liked this job, just as his mum had said he would. He didn't like having to hand over his wage packet to her each week, to be given his paltry dinner money and fares each day. The Lowthers in Penzance had taught him the unimagined idea of *saving*.

'Next year, when I'm fifteen, if I get a raise, I'm not telling her.'

She found out.

'Next year, when I'm sixteen . . .'

'Next year . . .'

'Next . . .': eighteen and National Service.

From pasty-faced, scruffbag urchin, Robert's flowering was majestic. At five foot nine he was not what you'd call tall, but perfectly sculptured. Lean and dark, with tweedy eyes and thick long lashes, he was sinewy, sexy, and smart. Not always smart enough to foil Mary, but better than Flo, Doll, and Win had been. Vi didn't count, she was untameable: no one got the better of Vi.

Away again, away from the family, to discipline, order, and a chance to save. He would get begging letters in Egypt asking for money. He would send back a postcard of palm trees. Mary wasn't going to give in. She could and would humiliate him across continents. She wrote to the army about him not writing home, not sending any money when he knew she was in dire straits, had a severe illness and babies to look after . . .

He didn't need to be shown her letter, he could smell the lyrics from across his commanding officer's desk.

After a military bollocking he did as he was ordered and wrote home.

Dear Mum and Dad,

I enclose a money order for five pounds. I will send you a money order for five pounds every month. Please don't bother to reply, I hate getting letters and so does my CO, thank you very much. I'm sure you will make a speedy recovery from your severe illness the moment you are able to cash this.

Robert Roberts.

His life with Mary, his time in Cornwall, and now two years of army life were beginning to join the dots up for Robert. He found that there was more of him, a bigger, funnier, smarter him, in the away-from-the-family world. The army had brought out the Mary in him. He would take her on, head to head, and she wouldn't know what had hit her.

He went back to his old job, this time keeping his wages to himself and giving her, after some hard bargaining, enough for his food, his bed, and his washing. Through night school he had friends that none of the family ever saw, secret girlfriends. At night school he learned plumbing and gas fitting. He did more or less what he wanted and, to his surprise, got away with it.

Robert was going on his first holiday, to Butlin's holiday camp in Skegness, with three of his mates. One of the boys had taken charge of collecting the money each week. It had taken six months, but now they were all paid up and ready for the luxury of nothing to do but lark about, swim, dance, drink. And girls, girls.

Robert had allowed himself ten shillings spending money for the week. He'd hidden this one note from Mary by flattening it out and pinning it to the top of his bedroom door, making sure that the door could still open and close without creating interest. It had to live up there for two weeks. Each night before bed, and each morning before work, he would check on its existence.

With his case packed, his coat on, reaching up for it – he couldn't believe it. How Mary had found it, he never discovered.

She denied it, of course.

Robert made it. He had ticked all the boxes on his list: his own business, his own house, membership of the Masons, golf, marriage to a nice quiet girl from five miles away in genteel Ilford. She got an extra big tick for having not a speck of any of his sisters or his mother in her. And a son.

His house was on the far east outskirts of London – too difficult for any of the family, let alone his mother, to turn up and ask for anything. Robert didn't cut the cord completely. When George left school, Robert gave him a job as a plumber and helped him on his way.

Christmas time was when the whole family would meet up at Mary and Bob's to eat and fight and argue. Robert dreaded it. Most years he would pop in to see his mum and dad, give them a fiver, and be gone before the rest of them arrived. Occasionally, Doll would nag him enough and he'd give in and stay.

It was always awkward. Mary and Bob were careful and danced attendance on him, which irritated the life out of Vi and Win. Win hardly spoke to him at all, or he to her; they tried to keep out of each other's way. Robert had long forgotten why this should be. They had been so close as kids.

Win would never forget why.

'Get that little bastard out of here . . .'

Flo would be there some years and he would be pleased enough to see her, though now she was disappearing for long stretches. By the mid-1960s she was gone for ever.

'She went where?' Robert asked Vi.

'India, with Ali Box.'

'Who the fuck is Ali Box?'

Vi filled them all in with the recent life of Flo. Doll and Win knew some of it. Carol knew more of it, and Mary knew all of it. Bob decided to hear none of it and went for a quiet time in the lav.

'She's been living with Ali on and off for the past couple of years, not far from me. She met him through my Korim, so you can all blame me if you like. Ali Box is at least – what? eighty-one, eighty-two? – and wanted to go back home before he died. Wanted our Flo to go with him. We told her it wasn't like South-end, with fairground rides and candy floss. That it was baking hot, had tigers roaming about and that, but she wouldn't listen.

Someone said, '*Eighty-one?*'

'Anyway she's been gone for nine months now, and not a dicky bird. My Korim sent telegrams and everything. His brother's just got back from there, and no one has clapped eyes on either of them. They've had these terrible floods, hundreds of them dead and what not, so the upshot is, she must be floating down the Ganges with the rest of them.'

'First bath she's ever had, isn't it? The shock must have killed her,' said Carol.

'She's done what?' Robert could hardly hear over the music.

'Don't. None of us have met him yet.' Carol was laughing and jiving, spinning Robert around and swinging herself under his arms.

The band stopped thumping and they sweated back to their table. Robert glugged his beer and Carol sipped at her gin and tonic.

It had been a very good night. His clients liked her; they were completely charmed by her. Carol knew how to sing for her supper.

His wife was too quiet and shy to be any good on these business occasions.

'But what does she want to get shacked up with another one for? I mean, Korim was quite a nice one when you got to know him. Why she married that other article – what was his name? – I'll never know,' Robert said.

'This one's called Radge. Spelt Raj. The last one was Fahir,' Carol told him.

'Raj?'

'If you meet him, just think of Raj, Taj, and Bobtail. That'll remind you.' Carol gave him a saucy look and went off to the ladies.

He loved to see her happy and prettified up to her best. For years she would be his 'date' – and if she had a black eye or a bruise, Doll would be her stand-in.

It was the phone call to Big George that started it.

'This is my only shilling, boy, so I'll make it snappy. We never got our coal this week and me and the old man are freezing our nuts off. I quite understand if you can't afford it any more, you know I don't want you to go short yourself because of me and your dad. We would hate to do that to you, son . . .'

George stopped her in her tracks. 'Well, me and Robert have been paying for it. You sure it's supposed to come today?'

'Yeah, course. I know when it's due and when it's not because I eke it out, don't I? So it will last for us. I'm sorry to drop this on you, boy. I'm sure this is all you need, me begging for . . .'

The phone went dead. It was ten o'clock at night. George imagined his mother walking back in the cold and dark from the phone box to the small basement flat in Plaistow, two streets away.

He rang Robert.

The two brothers then had a row about who had last paid the coalman. George was supposed to pay one month, Robert the next.

They decided the only way to get to the bottom of it was to go to the coal merchant's first thing in the morning.

Yes, the coalman told them, he'd delivered five hundred-weight last week, and yes, they'd paid for it.

That was more than enough to last another three weeks, so why didn't she have any coal?

She'd sold it to her neighbours, a bucketful at a time.

Robert considered putting in central heating in for her, but it wasn't worth the aggravation. You never knew when she would be on the move again.

Boxing Day 1956

'I'll be calling yo-o-o-ou, you-hoo, you-hoo ...'

'Will you answer to-o-o, oo-hoo, oo-hoo?'

They had ladies' turbans on with tin curlers sticking out at the front, smudged orange lipstick, Aunt Vi's eye-black pencilled round their eyes, and their trousers rolled up as high as they would go.

Dad and Uncle Len were singing and dancing together in the middle of the room, doing silly pointy-toes ballet shapes in their socks, while Granddad played his squeezebox. The dining table had been pushed against the wall to make more room, and the chairs were lined up in a tidy row so we could all watch the performance.

We were laughing, clapping, and Aunt Doll and Aunt Vi kept pointing their toes and trying to trip up Dad or Uncle Len.

Big George started off, then we all joined in, us kids the loudest: 'You can't sing at all, at-all, at a-a-a-ll.'

Mum was dancing with Buster, I was dancing with Ron, then Big George and Little George rolled their trousers up like Dad and Len. The men always dressed up as ladies at Christmas.

When everyone had 'you-hoo'-ed themselves silly, Uncle Len flopped exhausted onto a chair.

'Gawd help us, give us a beer, Doll,' he said.

Dad was still prancing on his own.

When he'd got his breath back, Uncle Len picked up his

accordion from the floor and joined Granddad in playing something very slow and whiny. Uncle Korim beamed as if this was a happy tune – maybe he was just happy that we had stopped howling and wailing.

'Bill, are you going to wipe that off or are we going to have to get on the bus with you looking like that?' Mum shouted.

'I don't know what to do for the best here,' Nanny was saying.

There was a lot of mooching about going on: a long queue for the lav, cups and beer bottles being taken back to the scullery, and coats being sorted out. Buster had been given a clean bum before we left for the buses home, and Lionel was being winded.

'What if you sent our Flo round there? Couldn't she make some excuse or other, make sure everything's hunky dory?' asked Aunt Vi. Uncle Korim caught my eye, smiled, and wobbled his friendly head.

'Me and Len could pop in on our way back, we could say we just wanted to see her and the babies and wish them a happy New Year and that.' Aunt Doll obviously thought she and Uncle Len would be a much better option than Flo.

'No, I reckon it's best left for tonight. Whichever way we handle it, we're going to be in the wrong. If you leave her be, you've got more of a chance of having a word on the quiet when she does come back.' They 'umm'-ed and 'ah'-ed, but in the end agreed with Mum.

'If a man ever raised his hand to me . . .'

Why did they all think that the Galoot had walloped Carol? She said she had hit her head. Why were they making a mountain out of a molehill?

'I'll sit up tonight until she gets back, all right? Then I'll phone you in the morning, Doll, and tell you what's been going on. Then you two can phone Doll, say about eleven? How's that?'

Mum and Aunt Vi listened to Nanny's orders, thought for a bit, and nodded.

We waved off the Harrises in their shiny black car. Aunt Doll was in the front, smiling and waving slowly like the Queen does, with Ron and Barbara copying her from the back seats.

More shivering kisses and cuddles on the pavement and we were off.

'It's fucking taters out here, we're going in. Ta-ta, you lot.' With that, Nanny pushed Granddad, Flo, and Pattie back down the basement steps. Big George was nowhere to be seen.

CHAPTER TWELVE

Carol

She was gorgeous: pale skin, green eyes, and a mass of complicated red hair – a cheeky little figure with a temperament to match, like a Shetland pony. She was pregnant. Would he marry her? He wouldn't be given a choice in the matter.

It could have been Mary forty years earlier.

The red hair wasn't as complicated as it might have been in 1915; this was June 1954 and Carol was fifteen years old, with a fashionable little bulbous perm, and soon to have a little round belly. She wouldn't be sixteen until October. Mary and her youngest daughter were sitting on the front step of Salmen Road, waiting for Bob to get home from work – best to tell him the news out in the open, where he would be unlikely to cause ructions.

When Mary told him, all he said was, 'Here we go again.'

He looked at his baby girl and thought of all those histories. Then he looked at Mary and saw the terrible damage that time had done.

High fertility – or carelessness – brought Carol three babies before she had finished her nineteenth year. She married Tony Cooper three days after her sixteenth birthday, four months before the first baby arrived. Tony was also sixteen. He was tall and gangly, fair-haired and fair-eyed. He worked hard to look like an American, a rock-and-roller, with a quiff bending forwards from his low forehead.

Carol's story can never fully be told. She didn't know the extent of it herself for thirty years. Mary and Bob were dead before drips of the crime turned to hailstones. This time the Roberts family was completely innocent.

'I'm going to have to help her out, poor little cow. She's got herself knocked up again,' Mary told Vi, Doll, and Win. The three daughters would meet up on Friday mornings at their mother's. Win would be there because she had to; she had to go to Stratford Town Hall every week to pick up her fifteen shillings' maintenance for Roberta. She had never wanted to take Robert Alexander Archer to court, but Mary had made her do it years ago – that or have her baby adopted.

'If she don't want it – to have it, I mean – send her to me. I know someone who can help her out,' Vi said.

'Oh, do leave off, Vi. Haven't they heard of Durex, for fuck's sake?' said Win.

'Don't you get on your high horse, madam,' Mary chimed in.

Doll called a halt to the proceedings, tea was made, fags were lit, and they discussed the Carol situation. She, her baby, and trainee hairdresser Tony were living in one room of his mother's house, a rented three-up two-down little place in West Ham, two miles away from Mary.

'She don't like it there, there's not enough room and, to put the tin lid on it, that shifty brother of Tony's keeps making eyes at her the minute Tony's back's turned. We've got to get her out of there. So, my reasoning is, I get a bigger place, they all come and live with me, share the rent, and I can look after the babies while she goes out to work.' The three sisters were silent, waiting for the next instalment.

'It wasn't easy, I've had to walk my fucking legs off, but I've found somewhere that'll do.' They knew this was no longer an idea fermenting, this was a cut-and-dried fact. 'I've not let on to the old man yet – and don't you let on if you bump into him. It's a big house, just over the station bridge and across the main road. There's a basement, two rooms, and a kitchen they can have, and me and the old man, our George, and Pattie can have the upstairs. It's got three bedrooms up there – so, ideal, isn't it?'

That is exactly what happened. Mary charged her daughter the full rent for the basement, and Mary and Bob, along with George and Pattie, lived in the bigger part for free. Flo would come and go.

Tony Cooper's trainee hairdresser days were well and truly over. The Roberts family more or less ordered him to grow up and get a man's job. His brother-in-law, Robert, had tried him out in the heating and plumbing business, but he was cack-handed and hopeless. He tried plastering, labouring, and finally turned to Win's husband, Bill, who was an asphalter. He got his man's job, boiling up the asphalt to spread on the roads. Carol went temping as a filing clerk between pregnancies.

By April 1958 they had three children under the age of five: Gary, Tracy, and now Ray. Tony and Carol weren't quite twenty. The two youngest of these three children would suffer a secret so bad that it was beyond any of their imaginings.

It was Tony's big success story: a secret that would be kept for thirty years.

Carol made sure that she didn't have any more children with Tony. Whether Vi 'helped her out' now and then, no one was saying. The children went to school and Carol got a job as a dental nurse. She saved some, she borrowed some, and she got into debt some, buying a little house a ten-minute walk away from Mary's and a few streets away from her mother-in-law. Both grandmothers could help with the child care.

Tony Cooper turned to lard and dullness before he'd reached his early twenties. His best friend was his elder brother, and the two of them were interested in motorbikes, jiving, and sleeping.

He wasn't that clever at the asphalting – he was slow and clumsy in a job that required a certain amount of speed and deftness – but Tony was too brain-stodgy to notice that most days Bill covered up for his mistakes. This barely literate plank, adored and spoilt by his mother and brother, didn't have a clue as to how ignorant he was. It didn't cross what could only loosely be called his mind that he was tolerated by the Robertses just so long as he kept his filthy mitts off Carol and the children. The family had no idea that they ignored him at their peril.

Carol became more ravishing and inquisitive about everything around her, though not more confident – Tony made sure of that. She dreamed of stretching out and feeling the world – dreamed it had to be bigger, richer, and more muscular than London E13. This house, this job, were merely a caress.

Any social life she did have revolved around visiting her brothers and sisters, almost on a rota system. Each one gave her something different. Flo was invisible, of course; there was an age gap of twenty years, and a vital discrepancy in grey matter, between them. Doll was the dream mum, soft and emotional. That was where Carol would run when she was fearful. Vi was funny and dangerous, hard as nails, and knew all sorts. Carol would run to Vi when a secret needed to be kept and morality was not on the agenda. Win was serious and distant and not that interested in her, on top of which Win made it clear that she didn't like Tony much, so visits there were few and far between.

Big brother Robert wanted more for her. He hated his little beauty being tied to kids too early, tied to the Galoot, the new family name for young Tony – a label to join the long list of family insults.

Robert started to take Carol to his business dos – partly to give her a bit more fun, partly to keep her out of trouble, partly to give her more confidence, but most of all to show her off. She liked men and men liked her. With Robert's money she learnt how to dress quietly sexy, to amuse the Masonic movers and shakers that made up Robert's non-domestic life.

Tony Cooper got duller and duller, and to flex his muscles would beat Carol up from time to time.

Everyone had their own opinion about what was going on. Doll would think Carol must have pushed the boat out a bit, but that he shouldn't have hit her. Vi would think, along with Mary, that maybe Carol had got a bit careless and perhaps deserved a good hiding. Win would think that she should leave him immediately. When a man hits you, that's the end – finished.

The first time Robert and George got to hear about it, they went and gave Tony a good talking to, with serene threats of castration if he ever did it again.

They should have castrated him.

Tony hit her – a lot, below the belt where no one could see, except perhaps a lover or a doctor – trying to punch the sex out of her. Her children watched all this and learned from her to keep it a secret. That's what he wanted, that all of them should tolerate him in silent fear. He didn't tame her, but he disciplined her in a way that he could never have imagined. When he hit the children, she could work out his level of menace from the amount of dribble and saliva produced. If he was dry-mouthed and hollering, she would let it carry on until he got fed up or the children stopped moving. When it got too dangerous, she knew there was no way out but to stop him with a blow from a chair a clock – anything to make him turn on her.

She offered him this pretend power over her as she grew further and further away, and he was too doltish to see through it. She was very frightened of him, but not completely cowed. Sex and food would relax his fire, and tomorrow held the promise of another day.

Watching Tony slurp the brains out of a sheep's head, his absolutely favourite nosh, made her and the children feel as if their own brains and lives were being sucked down his gullet. Carol didn't have the stomach to cook this delicacy and would ask Mary to do it for her – to buy it and roast it – and Carol would collect it on her way home from work. This decapitated dinner would be kept warm for him in the oven while she cooked something more palatable for herself and the kids. On his arrival she would serve it up as though it were caviar.

'When these kids are teenagers, I'm gone, away from this.' She needed to speed up their lives.

Meanwhile, Tony was making a better job of it than she ever could.

'Doll? Oh, Doll, you've got to get over here now, it's our Carol. That fucking Galoot, he's gone haywire. I don't know what she's supposed to have done, but the poor little cow doesn't deserve this.'

Click, and Doll was on her way to Mary's.

'Robert, get your coat on and get over here, and go via our Vi's and pick her up and bring her here, she don't have a phone . . . I know it's a fucking long way round. I've got her three kids in a right state here. Cooper's nearly done her in this time.'

Click, and Mary made another call.

'George? I need you to do something for me right away. Get over to our Win's, she's not on the phone, and tell her something has happened to our Carol . . . I don't know myself yet, boy, just tell her that Tony has given her more than a good hiding this time . . . No, I don't need you here tonight, but I do need you to tell Win and then we can all meet up here tomorrow to find out what's what . . .'

Within the hour anyone who was on their way had arrived at the basement in Maud Road. Seeing the comings and goings, the upstairs neighbours were preparing themselves for a Roberts family shindig and no sleep.

The grown-ups stared at Carol's three children, who were quiet and still and pale. You could have believed that they were sharing one breath between them to keep alive. It was 1965; the youngest was only seven years of age and the eldest had just reached eleven. It was nearly midnight.

When Tony had finished his workout on his wife, he walked the few streets to his mother's and had a drink with his brother. Eight-year-old Tracy rang 999 and Carol was carted off. The children promised the ambulance men that they would stay with a neighbour. The minute the ambulance took off, they walked the mile to Nanny Mary's.

The family weren't sure where the ambulance had taken Carol, so they took a chance and went to the nearest hospital, Plaistow, at the end of their old road in Samson Street. It had once been the fever and smallpox hospital. Bob was told to stay at home with Pattie and put the children to bed.

Carol was there.

Robert argued, threatened, and generally threw his weight about. They were allowed to look at their sister through a window – not a pretty place, not a pretty sight. Her face was a round ball, black and blue, with a tube coming out of a slit that had once been a full mouth. Blood matted her hair, there was a tube in her arm, and a nurse was sitting with her, checking the monitors. Carol was barely conscious and had no idea that she was being watched by a silence of rage.

Doll wobbled and was caught by husband Len, which made the rest of them rally round and begin to think sanely again. Once the nurses had promised them that Carol wasn't going to die, they accepted the order to leave and come back in the morning. They went home to Maud Road and sat up all night, keeping an eye on anyone who might burst and go round to find the Galoot.

The news was good, they told Bob. She had a broken

cheekbone, collarbone, and arm, and severe abdominal and facial bruising.

The sitting-up all night had not been wasted. Robert organized a solicitor with a camera and Mary, Doll, and Vi gave Carol a lecture about never going back. And yes, the kids were fine, but they mustn't see her like this or they would never be able to forget it.

Someone knew someone who knew someone who needed money, and Tony was beaten up in his turn. He didn't seem to mind much. Carol had two weeks in hospital to make her plans. She had nowhere to go with the children – none of the family had enough room for all of them. The kids went back to Tony and their schools and the mortgaged home that she had had such high hopes for.

The solicitor's photographs made for a simple divorce; that was one battle that Tony turned his back on.

Carol stayed with Doll and Len when she first came out of hospital, and Mary would bring the children over to see her. This was repeated with Robert, and then at Vi's. She had no home, no kids, no job, no money.

It took three months before her face looked like herself again, and her brothers knew she needed to get out and into her new world. They took her on business trips, gave her spending money, parties, found her a job.

Then she met Dougie. He was twenty-two, she was twenty-eight. He was shy, scruffy, partially deaf, a scrap-metal merchant working for his father, and he dreamed of one day having his own business. He wasn't Carol's usual type, but he had something she had never seen in large doses before. Devotion.

They rented a large house in Bethnal Green, near his family and about seven miles away from hers. Dougie had found this house; he would do it up himself and make it a palace for all of them. It didn't happen like that, though. She thought it for the best that the children, who had been living with Tony for the past year, with his mother's help, shouldn't be uprooted again. She could have them all school holidays, birthdays, and every other Christmas.

The children would never completely forgive her for that.

She fell pregnant – for the first time in her life, a happy pregnancy. Twins. They didn't survive more than a few hours. Had Tony damaged her for ever? Fertility won out, though, and over the next couple of years she gave birth to a beautiful daughter and, later, an adored son. She was older and wiser, and given this second chance she brought them up with money in her pocket and fun in the air. Dougie spoilt them tenderly.

Her three other children were growing into teenagers. The eldest, Gary, was the easiest to handle; he did steal and drive away a double-decker bus once, but that was all. Whereas Tracy and Ray clung to each other and no one could get between them. They ran away from time to time, stole trivial things occasionally, and sometimes cried for hours.

She had told them she would always be there for them, but she wasn't.

Carol thought they loved their father more than her, and they thought she loved her new children more than them.

Ray, the youngest child from her first round of babies, had received the information without it being in any way news. He was HIV positive. His partner, John, had died of Aids three years before and Ray didn't believe in miracles.

It was 1988 and the perfect time to spring-clean his harmed heart. Telling his sister Tracy would be hard. Would she believe him? She did, because she had been there. It was the only secret they had ever kept from each other, and now it was out, for them to tell and for the world to hear.

Tony Cooper would stand in the dock at the Old Bailey

accused of the sexual abuse of Tracy and Ray. There was a distinct aroma of something wrong about the later children he had fathered, but he would drop dead of a heart attack before the court had heard the full story. Ray had trembled when he stood up and faced this father. He would have run away, not been strong enough, if it had been only his own misery, but this was for both of them. Tracy needed him to splurge this out even more than he did.

'After going through all that and he still gets away.'

Tracy had to repair herself quickly because she now had three children of her own. It took Ray longer.

He saw his father's severed, baked head sitting on a plate. The top of his head sliced off. Ray dug in with his spoon and devoured that nothingness.

He never saw his mother again.

Perhaps Tony had spared the eldest boy, Gary, because he looked so much like himself. It might have seemed a bit like self-abuse.

It was the seriousness of the court case that woke Carol up to the damage Tony had done to the children, and to the fact that they must have been telling the truth – only by then it was a little too late. Ray died nine years later, with his adored sister at his bedside, and no amount of persuasion would convince him to let his mother see him.

Four years afterwards, Carol died at the age of sixty-three, with her gullet ripped out first by throat cancer and then by the surgeons. Her funeral told her life. Just two of her five children were there. Ray was dead.

There was Tracy, who had attempted a new beginning with her mother after Ray's death. Now grown up, with handsome children of her own, she was doing her best. So was Andrew, Carol's final baby, who was nearly thirty now, with his dad, Dougie. Both in their own trance of pain.

Who else of Carol's blood walked out of the cemetery?

Doll – only she wasn't walking, she was being pushed in a wheelchair by her god-daughter, Roberta.

Robert was there, walking alongside Doll and holding her hand. The pair of them were at a loss as to how this could have happened to their little sister.

No Flo, still floating down the Ganges.

No Vi, dead and buried three years before.

No Win, dead and burnt six years before.

No George, he was crying in New Zealand.

Boxing Day 1956

*M*ary poked the embers of the fire and chewed on the last piece of bread pudding. It was two o'clock in the morning. She had looked everywhere for him.

Sitting there in the dark, calming herself with the thought that George must have gone back round to his mate's house, she tried to concentrate on what should be done about Carol.

Mary won't get to bed tonight. In a half doze, she falls into that scary world of horror: George's broken, lifeless body dragged over the front steps by the Chinaman, his lost ivory teeth crammed into George's bloodless face. Mary twitched awake, heart pounding, listening for any noise from the street. She turned the light on, hoping that it would keep her alert.

Mary watches herself standing in court, the judge places a black cap on his head: 'Mary Burke, you will be taken from this place to a place of execution ...'

'Mu-u-um! Mu-u-um!'

She can hear George's voice calling her from a long way away. With the hood over her head and her hands tied behind her back, she can't help him, can't get to him ...

'Nanny, Nanny? You all right? Shall I light the fire, it's eight o'clock?' There was Pattie, shaking her out of her hell.

'Where's George? Have you seen George?'

'Yeah, he's gone off to bed. I let him in about ten minutes ago. Shall I make a pot of tea or light the fire first?'

Mary contemplated thrashing George for causing her night terrors. She was exhausted, the stuffing had split out of her. Instead, she lit a fag and waited for the tea.

CHAPTER THIRTEEN

George

'*C*ome back here, you little toerag.'

'Fuck off, you fat old cow.'

George, dripping and covered in tea leaves, scooted out of the front door and across the road to the bombsite.

Mary was standing on her doorstep, absolutely livid. He had wound her up so much, with 'Oh, go on, Mum, only threepence. Come on, you old mare, or I'll tell Dad about the tallyman,' that she had thrown a pot of warm tea over him and now she was left holding just the handle. The rest of the pot had come away in her hands, hit George, hit the deck, and smashed to bits.

Ten-year-old George stayed away for two hours, inside a nest made of three bits of corrugated sheeting. He didn't try and remove any bits of china or the tea leaves – he was saving them so his dad would feel sorry for him when he got home from work. She'd have to give him his threepence then.

He'd run Mary ragged. She was fifty-three and couldn't keep up with him. Bob thought he was just being a boy; he never saw the half of his chicanery.

George was too young to know the ins and outs of what his older sisters had been through with Mary, but he knew that, for reasons not yet clear to him, he had to stay one jump ahead of her. He hadn't worked out whether Pattie had been a born skivvy or whether Mary had manufactured her, trained her like a terrified imbecile. Whichever was the case, it wasn't going to happen to him, he'd make sure of that.

Win and Roberta had left Salmen Road, then Carol, and he couldn't bear it alone, so on Saturdays he'd stay all day with Carol and on Sundays go and get fed at Win's. It took three buses to get to Win's and he always managed to get away without paying. Sitting upstairs was the key. If he managed to catch Robert Alexander Archer's bus, he was home and dry.

'I'm Win's brother, Roberta's uncle. You used to come round our house, didn't you?' R.A. would blush, not take his fare, and carry on down the aisle, punching the tickets of honest folk. With unknown bus conductors, George would tell them that his mum had his fare and she was sitting downstairs, and at the next stop he'd jump off, get another bus, and skive all over again.

'Whatever have I done to deserve this?'

'God must be punishing you for something, Mary,' her neighbours would call out when they saw her screaming after him again. What drove Mary mad was that those who didn't have to put up with him found him funny. In the end she gave up and let him run riot. She had linen to sell and debts she worked hard not to pay. These days Pattie had become her regular donkey.

George grew up fast. He couldn't wait; it was as if he had been born with wings on his heels, never destined to be around for long, flitting for dear life. This Just William in short grey woollen trousers, grubby plimsolls, with occasional nits, grew speedily into a 'Just George', with drainpipe trousers, greased-back hair, and two false front teeth. They had been knocked out playing football. He was going to be a footballer – was going to be famous for having some sort of talent – anything to take him away from the exhausted grey light of London in 1959.

Mary and Bob were nearly sixty and feeling it. They needed George, now sixteen, to go out to work, not to play at no money dreams. So he was left with very serious amateur football on Saturday afternoons and learning the heating and plumbing business from his brother.

Apart from the teenage loss of his front teeth, George followed the family in the looks department. The girls loved him, this Adam Faith lookalike, with fair soft hair, the family cheekbones, large green eyes and long dark lashes, full mouth, square nose, and square, lean body. He could return an insult before the other person had quite finished, like his mother and his sisters.

Girlfriends would be made to watch him at football practice on a Wednesday night, be taken to the pictures on a Friday night, watch him play in the match on a Saturday afternoon, and then, after waiting for him to spruce himself up, they would be taken to Win's on the Isle of Dogs to play cards – for money, of course. They would stay the night on Win's sofa and get up to all sorts of things that you weren't supposed to do before 1963. On Tuesday and Thursday nights he went to night school. None of the girlfriends lasted more than a couple of weeks. He was unsettled, always on the helter skelter for more of something with so much energy that he thought he would burst into flames with it. The passion to reinvent himself came gradually, and he needed someone to help him break out of the egg of his heredity.

Patricia walked in and steadied him. She was strong and pretty and an accounts clerk. Good with money, he liked that. They were both eighteen. She didn't cry or get hurt by the fleetness of his tongue, she laughed and soaked him up. She even liked football when it wasn't raining.

'Where the fuck is he?' Mary asked Doll. Doll didn't answer and looked to her sisters for a clue. They didn't have one. Patricia and her father passed the church for the fourth time and told the driver to go round the block again. The bride's mother, along with fifty other people in various best suits and hats, fretted outside St Luke's Church, Stratford, hoping for a glimpse of George and his best man, Robert. All they knew was that the two brothers should have been together the night before for a good piss-up, and that George was to have stayed at Robert's and be delivered safe and sound to the church.

Patricia had made her mind up. One more circuit of the church and she was going home.

A black taxi almost collided with the bridal car. Three young men in snazzy grey suits jumped out of the cab, followed by Robert in a black business suit and George with a cut lip and mud in his hair. Patricia told the driver to go very slowly one more time round the block, to give her husband-to-be and his best man a chance to get down the aisle before her.

'Where have you been? We've been spitting feathers here, waiting and waiting, it's the bride that's supposed to be late . . .'

Robert didn't give Mary a chance to finish. He'd been playing football, it went to extra time. 'Get in the bloody church before her car gets back.'

Patricia and her tiny father eventually walked down the aisle to 'Here Comes the Bride'. Maybe the organist played it as slow as the Death March because he was fed up with the delay. The long, creeping haul towards the vicar gave everyone time for the usual 'ooh's and 'ah's over the bride's dress and the two bridesmaids. Patricia's long white imitation satin and lace gown wasn't the most expensive one that C&A in Oxford Street sold, but she had paid more than she had intended. She didn't want too low-cut a neckline and she needed sleeves. Demure loveliness was the effect she had been after. The bridesmaids' outfits, one for Carol's five-year-old Tracy and the other for Patricia's twelve-year-old sister, Barbara, had been made by a neighbour in peach synthetic satin, knee-length with capped sleeves. All their shoes had come from the Co-op in Stratford. They had looked as pretty as a picture an hour before, but Patricia's mascara had smudged with the crying and little Tracy had fallen over getting out of the hire car. She'd scuffed her white sandals, her knees had gravel dents in them, her hairdo had become unravelled, and some adult, attempting to be helpful, had managed a fag burn in the back of her frock. The peach synthetic satin melted onto her skin, but further damage was prevented by Doll, Mary, and Carol all spitting on it. Patricia's Barbara looked lovely, ironed and hairsprayed into an almost immovable package.

George, best man Robert, and the vicar waited and waited while the organ droned on. George tried putting his face into a portrait of apology mixed with tenderness and love, but wasn't making a very good job of it. Whenever he made eye contact with Robert or the vicar, he chuckled with his mouth tightly shut. Patricia, determined to remain hurt and grave, stomped down the aisle. The vexed organist had changed his tune and was now banging out Purcell's Trumpet Voluntary. Patricia had put a spurt on and he couldn't keep up with her; neither could the bridesmaids, who had to burst into a trot. In the congregation Vi was reading the order of service, curious as to what this horrible piece of music was called. 'Trumpet Voluntary . . . ?' cackled out of her. Doll and Mary heard and just about managed to behave themselves.

Patricia breathlessly met up with George at the altar, looked at him, and burst out laughing. The organist still had quite a lot of music left to play, but, seeing that the bride had arrived at the altar, gave up in mid-trill. His hands hovered in the air for a second before he smashed them down again into an enormous off-key crescendo. The congregation clapped and the vicar looked cross. The Reverend Thomas dealt with the wedding formula as quickly as he could – 'Will you, George Victor

Roberts ...?' 'Will you, Patricia ...?' – and then came more music. As the second verse of 'Jerusalem' started up, the vicar shouted the next part of the service over the music. The organist got the message and stopped playing. Nobody was singing anyway. The Roberts tribe were all looking at Win waiting for 'And did those feet in ancient time ...'

Mr and Mrs George Roberts walked down the aisle to the Trumpet Voluntary again. It was a very speedy, upbeat version this time. Halfway down the aisle, Patricia caught her new sister-in-law Vi's eye and the laughter erupted again.

'What's going on? Am I missing something?' asked George.

For a while Patricia couldn't speak. Outside in the open, with the photographer taking ages to snap anything, lining up and arranging everybody, she told him: 'I just heard your Vi ask Doll if the Trumpet Voluntary had been written especially for your dad. Sorry, I kept thinking about it through all the serious bits. I'm not quite sure if I've just got married or not. I think the vicar might have heard as well. Oh, look, quick, smile.'

Everyone was gasping for food and drink; they had had enough of the church and the photographs and started to dawdle off down the road to the very new community hall. George, Robert, and Patricia did one more photo and joined them. There was lots of jollity once the booze hit the spot, some crying from miserable, tired kids, and just the one fight, between one of George's mates and Carol's Tony.

The music, provided by a local band doing covers from Lonnie Donnegan to Marty Wilde, drowned out most of it. The Galoot was sent home to his mother. After the fracas, Win's husband, Bill, and Doll's husband, Len, pinched handbags and hats off the ladies, rolled their trousers up, and put lipstick and eye-black on. While the band were having their break, Len and Bill belted out 'I'm gonna sit right down and write myself a letter and make believe it came from you ...' in high falsetto voices. The grown-ups laughed, the toddlers were frightened, and the teenagers went outside for a snog and a fag. A great time was had by all.

It was 1961 and finding affordable accommodation in London was almost impossible. George and Patricia were too young to have got a mortgage, even if they had had the money, which they hadn't, and they weren't eligible for council housing. The only other option was illegal – paying 'key money' for a council flat. This involved finding a council tenant who had moved on somewhere else without giving the flat back to the council. The tenant may have remarried and relocated out of the borough or even the country. 'Key money' of about two hundred and fifty pounds would be handed over for the 'key', and the new tenants would pay the weekly rent in cash. Building up rent arrears was not an option in this scenario: you had to be as invisible as possible.

The two of them moved into a one-bedroom flat in a Victorian tenement in Bethnal Green, just a mile and a half from the City and about seven miles from Plaistow and Mary. George's friends had helped him spruce it up a couple of weeks before the wedding. They wallpapered the bedroom and sitting room exactly the same, in bright orange with a large green leaf design. If you stared at the walls too intently it would make your eyes wobble. Patricia thought it looked like a pub. The tiny kitchen and lavatory were papered in a shiny plastic pine effect. They didn't have a bathroom, which was not a problem as the local bathhouse was only a ten-minute walk away. Patricia would have her bath on Saturday mornings, and George would rarely bother since he got to shower most Saturday afternoons after his football game.

They had saved hard to buy a double bed and two armchairs. These were purple velour with a grey stripe, and George hadn't taken their colour into account when he had chosen the wallpaper. The rest of their little nest was supplied by the wedding presents. They had some cutlery, crockery, tea towels, and a pair of lilac nylon sheets with pillowcases to match. The sheets came from Mary, who hated the newfangled material, but there was no market for good linen these days – it took ages to dry and was a bastard to iron, and people didn't have the time for that any more.

George continued working for Robert and Patricia kept her book-keeping job at a timber yard in Stratford. Her mum lived round the corner and she would go there for her lunch break just as she had done when she was single. For the next four years Patricia worked and saved and dreamed of motherhood and a house in the suburbs. George worked, played football, met up with his mates most nights, met girls, and dreamed of another life.

The longed-for baby arrived, nearly killing Patricia in the process. Twenty-two hours of labour, a tug-of-war forceps attempt, and finally a Caesarean released their healthy big son. Another George. Called Little Little George.

The house in the suburbs didn't materialize because George had the Robertses' DNA of the unfaithful in him. When he got married it was not to settle down but to settle out – out of the orbit of Mary and her cycle of endless poverty. He needed to be out of reach to be free.

'New Zealand? What about my mum, my family, my mates, your mum and everything?' Patricia stopped feeding the baby and couldn't believe her ears.

To be on the safe side, he would find a job and a home first and then send for them. His trip to New Zealand wasn't taken that seriously by the rest of the family. Mary, Bob, Robert, and the sisters treated his departure as if he'd gone for a packet of fags and would be back soon. It was a few months before it dawned on them all that they hadn't seen him in a while. They still expected him to walk in the door one day as if nothing had happened. Two years later Patricia and Little Little George were sent for.

He'd gone for good – or bad.

Patricia, frightened and lonely, couldn't wait to see him again and for the three of them to be together for ever. The news was good: lovely weather, rinky-dink bungalow of their own with a garden, lots of work as a plumber, peace and quiet, no blacks, and good schools. After the wrenching goodbyes, Patricia and Little Little George were gone.

The story unfolded slowly as all the witnesses were in New Zealand. Letters took weeks to arrive and phone calls were expensive and few. Robert got a call. When he saw Carol a week later, she was the next to know. Carol waited till she saw Doll, which took another week. Doll told Win, Vi, and Mary another week later when they all met up for their Friday yak at Mary's.

'She coming home then?' Mary asked her daughters.

'Mum, he's on the fucking missing list. He could be dead or whatever.' Win sounded agitated and could sense more pain coming. She could see her little brother being buried and forgotten by strangers.

'What are you talking about, dead? Course he's not dead. He's done a runner, hasn't he? I'm more worried for our Patricia. What's she going to do?' said Doll, trying to work out what should happen next.

'He'd better not show his face round here. He'd better not think he can come crawling back to me,' Mary said.

Doll, Vi, and Win looked at their mother, looked at each other, and fell into the first laugh of the day – as if! After a beat, even Mary laughed at herself.

Bob walked in carrying five portions of double pie and mash, followed by Ginge, his half-crippled ginger mongrel. Win went down the passage for a quick piss in the scullery, which was now en suite, and then to fetch the plates, spoons, and forks. She washed everything all over again, just to be on the safe side.

Back in the front room, Doll helped Win to dish out the pie and mash, while Bob was told the news.

'Who? Our George? He's done what? How d'you mean?'

The women overlapped each other between mouthfuls to tell the story: 'She's only been there six months, poor little cow ... hardly knows anybody ... She's round at dinner with little George as well ... someone he works with, his house, wasn't it? ... Yeah, this mate's missus is there an' all ... No, what did she tell Robert? About three couples were there ... they're all having a laugh and what not and our George suddenly says he's popping out for a packet of fags ... and that's it. Gone. Never seen again. What is it now, Doll? Three, four weeks he's been gone?'

'Well, has he had an accident? Police involved and what not?' asked Bob, trying to take it all in.

'Well, apparently the next day Patricia had a visit from one of George's mates who had been at the dinner, saying that George had phoned him to say that everything was all right, to say he's very sorry and he's in Australia. That Patricia must do what she thinks is right for her. To forget about him, it's for the best.' Doll finished her little paragraph with a resigned nod of her head.

Win said, 'Well, if this mate's telling her the truth, it sounds to me like they were in on it. Like they were all prepared for it. I'll write to her. That's all we can do really, I suppose.'

'He'll turn up. When he's ready,' Vi chimed in.

And he did. Two years later.

Walking down the basement steps to Mary and Bob's front door in Plaistow, he wondered what his reception would be – whether Mary would even answer the door at all, thinking it would be a tallyman calling for his money. Would Mary and Bob have their teeth in? He hadn't seen them in nearly five years.

'Hello, Mum.' Looking along the passage he could see that nothing, absolutely nothing, had changed, except that things were a little bit grubbier.

'Oh, hello, boy, wasn't expecting you. Run up the top and get us a packet of fags before they shut, will you?'

That was his homecoming.

He visited his sisters and Robert, and joked about Mary's reception, but they didn't laugh. They let him know that they were in contact with Patricia by letter and knew what had been going on. They never asked him to explain himself, and he never offered.

He went back to New Zealand, divorced Patricia, who decided to stay out there so that Little Little George would know his father, and found how lonely freedom can be.

With some minor jiggery-pokery adventures in between – running a hotel in the Philippines with some woman he'd met, and some forays in Australia, with, of course, more women – he went back to his plumbing and heating career, built a successful company, got comfortably rich and settled down. He got remarried, to a woman his family have never seen, with three children that they have also never seen – apart from Carol who missed him so much that she tried to make New Zealand work for her; it didn't, and he was left out there on his own.

In 1974 Bob died. George didn't come.

In 1986 Mary died. George didn't come.

In 1994 Win died.

In 1995 Vi died.

In 2002 Carol died.

In 2003 Doll died.

George didn't come.

Before the sisters died, he told them he had stomach cancer. They all decided he was telling fibs.

Mary, Mary, you never trusted anyone, and neither did they.

Roberta

'*I* know that man, don't I, Mum?' Little Roberta, nearly six years old, whispered to Win.

Win smiled and said to the bus conductor, 'She reckons she knows you.'

When I had said what I had said, 'I know that man,' it had just plopped out; I didn't have any kind of story around the words or any meaning to them. I was nearly six. How could I? My mother's smile and her connection to this bus conductor put me outside their secret, and ever since that moment I have known that there is a very fine line between protection and betrayal.

As I hid in Mum's armpit, the long slow bus journey, the man's uniform, his voice, brought back jangled pictures of when we had lived at Nanny's house, before we had moved to this new place called the Isle of Dogs. This was the 'before' man. He used to come and visit me and Mum when everyone else was out. I thought he was some kind of policeman. I would have to sit with them for a long time, trying not to wee myself. He would ask me questions I don't remember, but I do remember nodding or shaking my head. I thought he had come to take me away. Mum would say, 'Don't just nod your head, say something,' but the only word I seemed to know when he was around was 'Hello'. He'd get up, pinch my cheeks, call me

'What a chubby chops, eh?' and give me a silver threepenny bit. I would have to stay sitting on my little wooden chair while Mum saw him out of the house. I could hear them whispering in the passageway – about me? Had I been naughty? Had I remembered to say thank you? Sitting there trying to pull my thumbs off was a good way of getting to the nub of the matter, a way of remembering words, other people's words, my words. You pulled hard at your thumb and a picture would come, then the picture would melt into language: get the picture, get the words, get the answer.

We now lived three bus rides away from Nanny and Granddad, George and Pattie. I memorized the journey. Any bus from outside Plaistow station, on *the other side* of the road, would take me to a stop called Trinity Church. Get off there and cross the big road to the right, then cross again to the other side of the other big road. Outside the dentist where Mum used to work is the next stop. Get on the number five or fifteen and go all the way to Limehouse. Turn the corner to the left and wait outside the Chinese grocer's where the little Chinese lady adds up on the abacus and wait for the number fifty-six and ask to go to Tooke Street. It was much easier the other way round because that way there was only one road to cross. I couldn't wait to be big enough to do it all on my own.

Every Friday we went to Plaistow, for Mum to pick up her maintenance from Stratford Town Hall, and then on to Nanny's. Aunts Doll, Vi, and Carol would nearly always be there as well. From time to time there'd be strange Aunt Flo, who never said anything. Pattie and George would be at school. I never went to school on Fridays.

I met Bill Marney twice before Mum married him. He was the biggest person I had ever seen, with the deepest voice and the loudest laugh. I can't remember leaving Plaistow for good. I can't remember the wedding. I know I was there because a long time ago I saw a photograph of my mum in a large yellow and brown tartan coat and black court shoes with Bill in a smart blue double-breasted suit, white shirt, and shiny tie and shoes. They had carnations in their buttonholes. And there is almost me, holding my mum's hand and folding myself into her lovely coat which smelt of sweet talcum powder and Wills' Wild Woodbines.

I do remember our new home. It was a flat in a big block with a large plaque on the wall to say it had been opened by Queen Mary in 1934. Three storeys of red brick and long white landings spread out from the central stairwell. On either side of the stairs each of the landings had four blue front doors. 'If it's all on the flat, that makes it a flat,' Mum said.

So why was where Aunt Vi lived called 'the buildings'? Maybe because her place didn't have these long landings it wasn't a real flat. Not everyone called them landings: Mrs Inkpen called them 'verandahs' – little Johnny Inkpen has got a verandah and verrucas.

The courtyard at the front had a big circle of concrete with a concrete pole in the middle of it, and smaller concrete poles on the outside of the circle. These were the washing lines. Washing was to be put out on Monday mornings and retrieved by one o'clock. Each tenant had to scrub their landing and stairs on a rota. If everyone on your landing was healthy this would work out at once every eight weeks. It was the done thing to do it for the elderly and the infirm. There was a great deal of snobbery about the cleanliness of one's landing and stairs. At the back of the building were two lovely gardens, one at each end, and in between a concrete playground where kids could skate, play hopscotch, doctors and nurses, but No Ball Games. Surrounding the entire little estate were poplar trees dotted about twelve feet apart. Poplar trees in the borough of Poplar – more new words for me.

Our door number was fifty-six – the same as the escape bus from the Isle of Dogs. Once in the door, the passage formed an upside-down L-shape. The first door on the left was the bathroom, with a bath and lavatory but no sink. Carrying on would take you to two rooms and the kitchen. The kitchen was on the left of the upside-down L, with a big butler-sink and a long wooden draining board with tall, green-painted cupboards above it, a cream stove with a plate rack over the electric rings, an old oak dining table, one wooden chair with a red plastic seat, and dark-red stone tiles on the floor. The narrow window overlooked the landing.

The larger of the other two rooms had brown and cream checked lino, raggedy at the edges near the door. Nanny's lino also had large bald bits and was a similar colour to this in places. Perhaps it had come from the same tallyman. Opposite the door were two enormous windows with sills fat enough to sit on and look down at the pretty gardens below. I'd never been this high up before and I became fascinated by the tops of people's heads. I was still too small to see the tops of people's heads even when they were sitting down. There was something else in this room I had never seen before. Instead of the hole where the fireplace should be there was a huge black iron stove with a door and a big pipe going up into the ceiling: a range. A 'range'. I kept wondering where I had heard the word before. I hadn't known it meant a big black fireplace.

'The Co-op's doing a lovely range of underwear, Doll, have you seen?'

I had heard Aunt Carol telling Aunt Doll about it a couple of weeks ago, before horrible Uncle Robert's wedding. I sat on my window sill and thought of a lovely range of underwear, of a lovely range of flowers, of a lovely range of coal . . . Anything to stop me thinking about tomorrow and my new school and new friends and a lovely range of teachers. I didn't want to go to

school on my own. If I couldn't go to school with George and
Pattie, I wanted to stay here with my mum and wait till Friday
when we could do the buses to Nanny's again.

'You all right, Rob? What are you sitting there thinking about?'

I looked at my mum and had that horrible feeling that she had
been there a long time.

'Asphalt,' I lied.

'Come here, come on and help me with the carrots and tell
me why are you thinking about asphalt?' She waited for me to
follow her into the kitchen.

'A S H . . . No, A S P H A L T,' I spelt aloud.

Mum turned round and said, 'How do you know that?'

'Dad wrote it down for me yesterday and I've put it in my
memory box.'

After their wedding I was told that Bill had to be called 'Dad'.
I'd never called anyone else that before and was shy about it, but
I loved saying it. Dad was an asphalter and always came home
smelling of burnt summer roads. My job was to take his big
work boots off as soon as he sat down.

'Come on, girl, pull! That's it, pull!'

I'd take the boots into the passage, squat on the lino, and
search for bits of hard, dried asphalt that I could pull off and
keep. I liked to hold a bit squeezed tightly in my hand, hoping it
would warm up and the smell would get stronger, almost
shoving it up my nose to get the full power of it. I licked it once
and it didn't taste like it smelt. I preferred the taste of coal, but
that made a mess of your face and lips. I grew out of coal and
into a passion for the blackest liquorice.

Mum took me to my new school and handed me over to the
headmistress, Miss Coates, who in turn turned me over to
seven-year-old Linda Brown. She was to show me the ropes and
make sure I drank my milk and swallowed the vile capsule of
cod liver oil every morning at half past ten. It was on this first

day that I realized there was some secret in my life. I didn't know what it was, but I knew it was there. At playtime all the kids were questioning me, the new girl.

I thought it best not to answer, in case I got my mum into some kind of trouble. I racked my brains to think of what I must be hiding. I knew it was somehow to do with Plaistow, Mum, the policeman who was really a bus conductor, and my new dad, I just couldn't fathom what the problem was.

I was surrounded by what felt like all the primary school children in the world, though I suppose there must have been about twenty of them. They were in a great hurry to get the low-down on me. I bent my head and looked at my boys' brown lace-up shoes. The other girls were wearing variations on black T-bar shoes or perforated T-bar sandals in either sage green or pale blue.

'Have got any brothers or sisters? . . . Where do you live? . . . Her shoes are boys' shoes, look' . . . 'Do you think she's English?' . . . 'Can you speak English?'

I looked up and nodded. I thought of telling them that I was really Princess Anne and there had been some kind of mix-up at the hospital all because my mum's the spit of the Queen. The Queen had let us have a few of her servants and it was the servants who thought that this would be the best school for me.

I decided to keep that secret up my sleeve for another time.

With only the three of us in the flat, my life had suddenly become very quiet. I was used to being invisible in Plaistow with all the comings and goings of the grown-ups, and Big George making enough trouble and strife for me and Pattie to be left alone.

I'd go to school – noise in the playground, then quiet in morning assembly, hush in class, more playtime noise and ruckus again – come home from school to just Mum and 'Lift your feet up, Rob, you're making noise for the lady downstairs. Come on, be a good girl. Here, look, I've got some lovely white butcher's paper. I asked him to wrap it up in extra just for you. I'm going to write "difficulty" and you have to find as many words as you can out of that one word.' Mum sits me at the kitchen table while she prepares her stew.

I stare at her word: dit ... fit ... dut.

'I don't like that word, it doesn't have any e's.'

Mum looks again at what she's written and laughs.

'Fuck me, I can't even do it,' she says.

She writes out 'teacher' so that I can have two e's: her ... each ... tea ... rat ...

She shows me how to spell 'ache' and I have to look long and hard at how that shape makes that sound, and then my dad's home. We hear the cough as he reaches our landing; after the cough comes a whistle and after the whistle he rattles the door knocker. I'm there, ready for boot duty. It took me a few years to realize that the whistle after the cough happened when he had won on the horses or dogs.

Boots off and it was time for dinner. He wanted to eat as soon as he was home. He would talk about asphalt and spreading and being the pot-man over the stew. Jim the spreader was too slow and Dad's pot would boil over, or they had pinched some great lead off the roof of the brewery they were working on. They got about a fiver each for the lead. 'A result,' he'd say.

Before 'Dad' I couldn't remember anything about mealtimes. Now it seemed my new life was dominated by food. Breakfast, porridge or toast. At playtime, milk and cod liver oil capsule. Two hours later, school dinner. You had to finish your plate, had to. There was usually some kind of meat pie, with gristly bits, mashed potato, and pease pudding. 'Afters' was some kind of steamed pudding, and thick custard with rubbery skin poured over it.

We had to walk in crocodile formation to the dinner hall, two blocks and three streets away from the school. Linda Brown would hold my hand at the head of the queue. Miss Ryan, our teacher, would be at the rear. The streets were quiet and empty. The men were all at work and mothers were at home, indoors – apart from Linda Brown's nan who lived opposite the dinner hall and would be sitting outside her front door in all weathers, gossiping or snoozing, with her black and tan mongrel lying at her feet. Linda Brown lived there with her nan and her mum. She had told me that her dad was dead. I couldn't say that because my dad was now Bill and he was very much alive. Was her dad dead? Were we put together because we were both children of the Queen? I was jealous of her, living with her mum and her nan and a dad who was dead.

'My mum said that your mum is married to Mr Marney and that makes your mum Mrs Marney so why are you called Roberta Roberts?' Linda asked me on the way to the dinner building.

I thought long and hard as to whether this was my moment to mention the slip-up at the hospital and the Queen and Princess Anne and everything, but didn't feel up to managing a long story because I was still trying to unravel the question myself. It had never occurred to me that my mum had changed into someone else. I stalled. I knew that whatever I answered was of vital importance to my life at this school and to my mum's good name.

'It's not really a secret, but a bit of a secret. I'll tell you tomorrow,' I whispered.

Her anticipation of tomorrow frightened me, almost as much as the plateful of food I was now expected to swallow. Miss Ryan walked up and down the aisle, making sure we were eating and not talking. I ate the mashed potato slowly, while planning how to make the other stuff on my plate disappear. I couldn't have my 'afters' until I had finished this plateful. I didn't want my 'afters' anyway. The other kids came back with theirs and Miss Ryan was telling me to get on with it, we haven't got all day. Somehow a piece of knotted, slimy gristle found its way into my mouth. I gagged and it was all over. All over the floor – my vomit.

I had been at the school just a week and now my life was finished. Everyone was looking at me with 'aagh's and 'Puke!'s and 'Miss, that's horrible. Look what's she's done.' I thought about death and how I had heard the grown-ups say, 'Well, it comes to all of us.' If it was going to happen to me, I might as well die now and get it over and done with.

I didn't die a drop-down-dead, 'When's her funeral?' kind of death, I died by losing my invisibility. I was enormously visible; my sick was more than visible. I thought, 'I'll get through today and die tomorrow. Why wait till I'm old like Nanny and Granddad?' The cook, a round lady with a white turban and two rollers sticking out of her forehead, came out of the kitchen, took me by the hand, and marched me to the toilets. I could hear the swish and spittle of criticism from the room as I left. In the lavatory she tried to clean me up using two of her tea towels.

'If I were you, cocker, I'd tell them you've been feeling a bit sicky all day. They might send you home. Will your mum be in?'

I had thought she was angry with me but instead I sensed the conspiracy of protection. It felt so good that I had to go and ruin it by crying.

The cook had a face like a suet pudding. Her eyes were two bits of brown meat poking through the skin. Her voice was croaky and tender, as if she had once been me.

'If you tell me what you don't like, I won't put it on your plate again. How about that for a bargain?' she whispered, as she wiped my eyes and nose with the towel, which smelt of my sick.

'I don't like eating. I like bread and potatoes,' I mumbled back to her. She stared at me.

'Tell you what. Tomorrow and every day after that, when you're queuing up, just give me a little nod or shake of your head and I'll try and give you what you think you can manage, all right?'

Although I nodded, I was seriously worried as to whether I was being set up for even more humiliation. She had warts in her eyebrows with grey hairs springing from them, which made me think of witches. Maybe my future death would come from falling off her broom. By the time she returned me to the dinner hall it was empty. All the other kids were lined up outside, ready to get back to school. The witch/cook told me to stay where I was while she went to speak to Miss Ryan.

I could hear the clanging of washing up in the kitchen getting louder and louder and louder as if the noise was coming to arrest me. The cook/witch – I kept changing my mind about her – had been given permission to take me home to my mum. All I had to do was worry about tomorrow.

Witch/cook became cook/cook. She kept her word and only gave me what I could 'manage'. Food at home was more do-able. My mum had worked out that if she piled my plate with potatoes, cabbage, and shreds of gristle-free meat we could have a calm time round the table.

Dad would shout if he saw me picking and prodding the meat, and I would have to listen to how lucky I was and what he had had to eat when he was growing up. When that happened I lost the power to chew. My mouth would open and the food would fall out of its own accord back onto my plate.

'Oh, for fuck's sake, what's up now?' He would look to my mother for an answer.

'Rob, come, don't be naughty. What's the matter?' She said it patiently, with that secret look in her eye that was just about her and me, that she was sorry she had messed up about the meat. She was letting me down. My look at her was exactly the same. I was letting her down.

I got into the routine of this new life through what I had to eat. On Mondays to Thursdays the usual school dinners were made swallowable by dear warty cook, and Mum did her best at teatime. On Thursday evenings the good life began; it was Dad's pay day – sweet night. He would come home with a bag of sherbet lemons, a bag of pear drops (Mum couldn't stand them, they took her breath away, she said), a dozen twists of liquorice, a bag of chipped chocolates, and some toffee which they had to bash with a hammer. On Fridays we went to Nanny's and had delicious pie and mash, and on Friday evenings we would have fish and chips – a day of rest from worry. Saturday was a day with sandwiches and cheese on toast while Dad listened to his horses and the football on the radio. We spoke in whispers so as not to disturb him while he waited to find out if this was his lucky day.

I was allowed out on Saturdays to take his bets to Mrs Dixon, the bookie's runner, who lived on the ground floor of our flats. I didn't know what these bits of paper wrapped around money meant, but I was told not to tell anyone where I was going – otherwise I would get everyone, including Mr and Mrs Dixon, into a right predicament.

'Her eyes they sho-one like diamonds . . . I thought her the queen of the land . . . Her hair, it hung over her shoulder . . . tied up with a black velvet band . . .'

It was a bright, nine o'clock Sunday morning. We were having fried eggs, bacon, and tinned spaghetti – an almost worry-free eating moment, so long as the eggs were not too snotty. We could hear singing coming from outside. Mum said, 'Hark. What's that?' There was the sound of street doors opening. Dad carried on with his breakfast while Mum and I went to investigate. I wasn't big enough to see over the landing, so I ran to the central stairwell where there was a large window and peered out.

Downstairs in the middle of the undressed washing lines stood a small old man in a woolly rumpled suit, singing his Irish heart out. Three landings full of housewives laughed and threw pennies at him. With a deep bow he collected his earnings and wrapped them up in a large checked hankie. Then a curtsy and he was off again.

'Her eyes they sho-one like diamonds . . . Bill! Come on now! Where's me little mammy's boy? Bill! Your old fella's here to ask your forgiveness . . .'

Dad came out and peered down at this glinty-eyed leprechaun. The old man's singing and shouting slowed down and faded into silence. To my left and right I could see more people coming out of their flats. They looked at the singer, who was looking at my dad. They looked at my dad and I followed the direction of their stares. My mum was now looking at my dad. His face had died. It was as white as the cleanest bits of his vest. It took a while for his lips to reappear from the inside of his head.

'What's the matter, Bill? Seen a ghost?' Rosie Inkpen shouted across her 'verandah'. Her thin voice pierced the stillness and life was wound up again.

'But like Christ I have risen and come to meet again my prodigal sonny boy,' the old man boomed up to Dad.

'Fuck off. Sling your hook, you silly old bastard, you're twenty years too late. Go on, fuck off.' Dad was shaking and his voice was louder than I had ever heard before, which took some doing.

The neighbours went inside and shut their doors, out of kindness I suppose.

'Boyo, I'm on me last legs. Me mortal coil is unravelling as we speak. At least give your old fella enough for a drink to take the fear out of it . . .'

Mortal coil. It had a wonderful sound. Dad disappeared inside our flat and Mum followed him. I stared down at this funny old man. He looked up and gave me a friendly wink and I thought he was going to start singing again. Instead he squatted down in the middle of the washing lines and started to cry.

I mesmerized myself into believing he was the Genie of the Lamp who had got old and lost his powers, that he had no home to suck himself back into. Then Dad came back out again. He flung down a bulging, knotted blue handkerchief. It hit the ground with a chink and jingle of money.

'Now fuck off. Show your face round here again and I'll set the law on you.'

Mr Emms had come round the corner at that moment with his barrow of winkles, shrimps, cockles, whelks, and watercress and thought at first that Dad was shouting at him, then he spotted the old man opening the handkerchief and counting out the money. Along with the coins I could see a pink ten-bob note.

Dad had given him a lot of money to make him go away and repair his mortal coil.

Like a magician, the money had somehow vanished into his person, the handkerchief was in the top pocket of his shabby suit; he performed a deep curtsy followed by a quick smart salute and was gone.

Mr Emms was too flummoxed to start shouting his usual Sunday morning 'Luvverly herwink-holes. Luvverly hercock-holes . . .' He was interrupted by a crocodile of Floods on their way to ten o'clock mass: Mrs Flood, followed by her eldest, William, then John, then Ann, then Patricia, and finally little Mary. I looked longingly at the perfect head of Ann Flood. Why wasn't I called Ann? I'm an Ann.

Dad's colour had returned to near-normal, and with his

breakfast well and truly ruined he was determined that his Sunday tea should not be. He chucked two half-crowns down to Mr Emms.

''Ere, Emmsy, I'll have a pint of them winkles, pint of cockles, and two bunches of cress. Down you go, Rob. Emmsy, the little'un's coming to fetch it.'

I flew down the stairs on my errand, excited to have five minutes on the ground on my own. I got there just as Mr Emms found his voice again.

'Come and get yer luvverly hercock-holes . . .' He had a gob that could deafen bats. Doors were flung open and the noise of other people's lives filled the courtyard.

Back upstairs, Mum was busy peeling potatoes for dinner. I could tell from her back that she didn't want to speak. In the living room Dad was scratching his chin really fast, as if he had nits. I sat on the lino in the doorway so that I could have a good view of both of them.

'Well, what do you make of that then, Rob?' Dad asked.

I pushed the corners of my mouth up with my fingers to make me look comfortable and happy and sort of tweaked my head from side to side to some invisible musical jig. I'd seen Uncle Korim do that whenever he was asked an awkward question. Mum came and gave me a raw carrot to munch on, hoping it would keep me quiet.

'I want you to learn something, girl,' Dad said. 'That scruffy old bastard, disturbing all our peace, well, he's my old man. My father. He treated my lovely mother like an old dishrag and the last time I saw him I punched his fucking bone-idle lights out. Never done a day's proper work in his pip. No matter what you do in your life, you work hard, treat people the way you want to be treated, and not the fucking way other people tell you to treat people. They are going to fill your head with all sorts of nonsense at school and it's your job to work out if it makes sense to you, any sense at all.' He then went on about Germans and Churchill and cannon fodder, and how if it was left up to the workers there'd be no wars and why should he kill some German for the sake of . . .?

I was lost.

'Dad, have you killed a German? Did you make someone dead who was alive before they bumped into you?'

'I don't know. I most probably have. I was following orders. Y'see, that's why it's all bollocks. If the Germans follow orders everyone says they're wicked and evil. If I don't follow orders I get shot for being a traitor.'

'Bill, for fuck's sake, haven't we had enough for one day?' Mum shouted from the kitchen.

I went and sat on the window sill with my carrot and wondered about killing. I looked at all the colours of the flowers in the gardens downstairs. Mr Deeks, the caretaker, looked after them: his 'pride and joy', I would hear the grown-ups say. Miserable old bastard, my mum called him – not to his face, of course. I tried to count the number of flowers, then the number of colours. How many shapes are there? How many names for them?

Mum came in with some almost blood-free butcher's paper and crayons.

'Mum, is a shape the same as a letter or a number?'

She frowned at me, put her hand on my forehead as if I was unwell, tutted and walked out. I knew she thought it was about what Dad had said and she was not best pleased.

I had told Linda Brown as promised why my name was different from my mum's. I made it as complicated as I could in order to befuddle and finally bore her to death.

I said that I had been brought up by my grandparents and that it was their name and now the law said it was too late to change it, and also that we were rather important secret people so she mustn't breathe a word. I added in the servants by saying we had a black slave and that his coffee-coloured children came and helped the family from time to time. We had to keep them under wraps as some people would like to kill them – I thought it best to cover all corners in case anyone saw Aunt Vi and Uncle Korim come to visit with my cousins. It kept her quiet. She breezed about the school with a smarty-pants smile, enjoying being the only one in on my secret.

I asked her if her dad had been killed by Germans and she said very quickly, 'Probably.'

I let it go, just in case. My dad might have killed her dad by mistake – you never know – a stray bullet or something.

I was very honoured to have the friendship of Linda Brown. She was the best-dressed girl in the school and I was the scruffiest; she was also powerful and popular. When school was over, so was Linda. I had to come straight home and might be allowed to play on the landing outside the front door, where Mum could keep an eye on me. Ann Flood lived on the landing below. I longed for her to come up and play. She didn't go to my school, she was a Catholic. She went to St Edmund's school with cocky little Veronica Hawkins who lived two streets away and was allowed to play anywhere she fancied. Mostly she fancied calling on Ann and taking her away from the flats.

'Oh, Win, you don't send her to school like that, do you?' Nanny's idea of a welcoming cuddle was more like an inspection. I'd give her a kiss on the cheek, then she would push me back with her arms outstretched and spin me round, giving me the once-over. All this was done while she remained sitting in her armchair.

It was Friday and Aunts Vi and Doll were also there. Nanny

was staring at my coat. Mum gave her mother and sisters one of her 'Shut up' looks. Nanny wouldn't. 'Look at it, it's all bald down one side. Who the fuck gave you this?'

This wasn't a secondhand coat. Mum had bought it brand new from the Co-op. It was a double-breasted green tweed coat with a half-belt at the back – not that dissimilar to one I had seen Princess Anne wearing in a picture in the *Daily Mirror*. My buttons were bigger than hers though.

Mum tried to explain what I did when I was on my own, walking to school or running errands. She said, 'She never does it when she's out with me.'

I wished that cousins Ron and Barbara were there, so I wouldn't be so conspicuous, but they had to go to school even though it was a Friday – no maintenance day for them.

'Tell Nanny why you do it, Rob. Come on,' Mum ordered.

'I don't do nothing. I don't,' I lied.

They went on and on about it – all this fuss because I liked to go to school or round to the shop with my right shoulder pressed up against the wall. When there was a gap I would run to find another piece of wall. I hated gaps. I wanted to be the wall. I wanted to be the bits between the bricks.

'And it's making your head tilt to one side, on the wonk,' Aunt Vi piped in helpfully. 'Have a look at her forehead, she's gone bald on that right-hand corner.' Mum was now well and truly pissed off.

All my coats up until I was about nine were frayed and worn on the right-hand side and I had a permanent graze on my right forehead.

My skinny mum was getting plumper and that was good news for me. I was going to have a brother or sister apparently, so while Mum and Dad made arrangements, I was sent back to live with Nanny and Granddad, Pattie and George, for a long time.

I didn't have to go to school any more, and Mum and Dad would visit me every weekend. I suppose I stayed there for about three weeks, back to the noise and rows and bread and dripping; licking out the crusty corners of Granddad's rice pudding which he'd leave for me.

On Fridays I went with Nanny to pick up the maintenance and we'd get pie and mash to take back for when Aunts Vi and Doll arrived. This particular Friday was different. The grown-ups sent me into the scullery to eat mine while they whispered in the living room.

'You finished, Rob? Oh, yes, there's a good girl.' Nanny was bringing the dirty plates in. I knew from her tone that my time in the scullery was over. She brought me back in by the shoulders and placed me on her lap.

'Your mum wants me to take you back home on Sunday. Is that what you want, or would you rather stay here with your old nan?'

'Oh, leave off, Mum. Leave the poor little cow alone,' said Aunt Doll.

For some reason my pie and mash had not quite finished its journey to my stomach and I had to concentrate very hard to keep it down. I never answered the question. Instead, I asked myself a different one: did Mum not want me back?

Suddenly I remembered when I was about three, in this house, seeing my mum race across the bombsite with a battered suitcase. She was crying and she hadn't looked back at me. She'd gone on her first real holiday. She sent a coloured postcard. She brought me home some rock.

I knew I was going to make a spectacle of myself because my eyes and teeth had started to sweat, so I jumped down off Nanny's lap and ran out to the front step. But Aunt Vi caught hold of me: 'Oi, what are you thinking about, darling?'

'Skegness,' I said, and carried on outside.

I could hear them saying, 'What's she on about?' 'Something's upset her?' 'It's hard to tell, she's such a miserable-looking little bastard . . . like her father.' The last comment came from Nanny.

I pretended to myself that nothing had occurred and the feeling went away. The pearly November day had put an extra chill on my spine, which helped.

Sunday arrived and Nanny, Pattie, and me took the three buses to the Isle of Dogs. Granddad was coming as well, on his motorbike. He had a sidecar which no one would get into because he was nearly blind and shouldn't have been driving at all.

Even though we didn't get on *his* bus to get a free ride, Nanny managed to dodge the fare on the first two buses. She had to pay on the fifty-six to Tooke Street.

The flat was different. There was a big pram in the passage and a baby crying and my dad singing. The room with the range seemed much smaller now: it had Mum and Dad's bed, my little bed, and a big cot in it. The kitchen had a washing line full of nappies. Everywhere smelt wet. The singing and the crying went together. Dad was pacing up and down with the baby.

'He's got a big head for a little'un,' said Nanny.

So here he was, my first brother: Billy boy, for ever called Buster.

Mum looked tired and very white; she kissed me with parched lips and then asked me to put the kettle on and make everyone some tea. Pattie came and helped me because there was something going on. Brutal whispers were coming from my mum and Nanny. Granddad still hadn't arrived.

'Maybe he's killed someone,' suggested Pattie.

I closed the front-room door so that no one could hear, but Dad in the bedroom was winding down his singing as the baby fell asleep, and when he walked in to join them, Mum stormed out and came into the kitchen.

'What? What's up now?' Dad shouted down the passage.

'Leave her, Bill, she's all right. Women get the hump after a baby. She'll be all right in a few weeks,' Nanny told him.

When Mum heard that I thought she was going to smash up the kitchen. The sugar bowl hovered in her hands for a moment and then she crashed it down onto the table. Glassy dust crunched into the lino. Pattie ran to the door and stopped breathing. Mum sat on the kitchen chair, exhausted, and as I went to give her a cuddle there was a loud rat-tat-tatting at the front door and the baby woke up and started screaming again.

'You two, go and let your granddad in,' Mum said as she went to fetch the baby.

'Cor blimey, he's got a pair of lungs on him, Bill,' Granddad said as he whipped off his motorcycle goggles.

Nanny was being especially nice to everyone and making Dad laugh; my Mum looked haunted and was very quiet. She made tea, of winkles, cockles, and watercress, followed by tinned oranges and cold custard. She didn't seem to eat anything and spent most of the time in the other room with the baby. I knew she was making excuses, but was not sure why.

'Come on, Winnie, bring the baby in here,' Granddad shouted to her.

She didn't answer.

Dad didn't seem to notice she was missing – maybe because Nanny was making him laugh about something to do with Aunt Flo, who was on the missing list again. I knew Aunt Flo was Pattie's mum, but it never crossed my mind whether all this talk bothered Pattie or not. She seemed to take no notice.

I thought of when my mum was missing and the agony of Skegness. Now she was missing in the other room, with this big-headed baby who was my new brother.

Finally Mum came in, looked daggers at Nanny, asked Dad for a fag, and told everyone that Buster was now sound asleep.

When all the food had been devoured and cups of tea and fags finished it was time for …

'… us to make a move,' Nanny said.

With coats on and kisses done, Nanny rummaged into her green sack shopping bag. 'Oh, blimey, I almost forgot. Sorry, Winnie, it's not much, but I got you something for the baby. I'll get something a bit better when I'm more flush. Tell you the truth, I've not paid for them yet.' Granddad was putting his motorcycle equipment on and didn't hear the last bit. She had made sure he hadn't.

She brought out from her deep bag a pair of cot sheets in pure Irish linen. The present was wrapped in clear cellophane and tied with an expensive-looking blue bow. A poisoned smile passed between Mum and Nanny, a rigid cuddle, and then Nanny was out of the door, followed by Granddad and Pattie.

Mum slammed the door behind them.

'Win, there's no need for this. The poor old cow hasn't got two ha'pennies to rub together and she's bought you that smashing present. What's up with you?' Dad asked.

'Well, I hope you've got some money, Bill, because I fucking haven't. So unless you dig a bit deep we're going to go hungry this week. I suppose I could try and pawn the poxy sheets she's palmed me off with,' was Mum's answer.

Then all hell broke loose, with Dad shouting and Mum trying to explain herself to him. Buster woke up again and started yelling. I decided to go and find out how you stop a baby crying, but Mum got there first. She picked him up, undid the top of her frock and started feeding him. She plonked herself down on the side of my bed.

'Rob, come here,' she said. 'Do you know what month this is?'

'November,' I said.

'Right, and what month is your birthday?'

'February.'

'That's right, and how old will you be then? You'll be seven, won't you? And that's grown up. I want you to think really sensibly before you answer me and tell me the truth, okay?'

I looked at her and worried that I might not be up to whatever task this might be. I nodded my Uncle Korim's Indian nod.

'Can you remember how many times you went with Nanny to the town hall? You know where I mean, where I pick up my envelope of a Friday?'

I nodded. I counted.

'Three, I think. Yeah, the first time we went with Aunt Vi who paid our fare and Nanny gave her the envelope, the second time we had to walk there and it was really cold, and the last time we got a bus there and back.'

'She gave Aunt Vi the envelope?' Mum looked livid.

I nodded again.

'And the other two times, did she get an envelope from the man behind the counter?'

'Yeah, and she opened it to buy our pie and mash. Aunt Vi paid the first time,' I told her.

Dad was standing in the doorway and heard it all. He looked as if he didn't believe me.

'Oh, come on, Win, why would she say he hadn't paid up if he had?' asked Dad.

'Because I know him and I fucking well know her an' all. She owes Vi, so what does she do? Takes my fucking money and gives it to her. Vi is just as bad, she knows full well that I rely on that fifteen bob a week. And here's me, silly knickers, waiting for three weeks' money that she's paid off some of her debts with – first Vi, then fuck knows who else. I need my head examined. Remember, we'd already given her a couple of quid to look

— 226 —

after Rob – and his nibs would never let me down with the maintenance.'

'Well, he let you down before when he forgot to tell you he was married.' When Dad said this she pursed her lips tightly together and looked at me for a long time. Then she said, 'Rob, go and clear the table for me, will you, darling? There's a good girl.'

Nanny was never allowed to collect the maintenance again. We stopped going to Plaistow on a Friday for a while. Mum organized the money to be sent by registered post – she'd rather that than Nanny lying to her again and causing ructions. It was nerve-racking for her when the post was late. She didn't fancy seeing Aunt Vi either, though the new baby brought her, Aunt Doll, Aunt Carol, and Big George over. Uncle Robert never came.

'Come on, Rob, get a move on or you'll be late for school.'

My face didn't feel like my own. I smiled inside my head, but my skin and bone didn't follow. My neck felt as if God had grabbed me and was dragging me away somewhere. I stared at Mum's back as she was changing Buster's nappy. She must have felt me there, in the doorway.

'Oh, blimey, don't do that, you made me jump,' she said. 'What are you pulling that silly face for? Come on, do your laces up . . .' Then it dawned on her that something was up. She took my head in her hands – her hands that were wide, cool, and soft.

'Poke your tongue out.'

I tried but couldn't remember how to do it. Well, I could, but my face wouldn't do as it was told. She didn't look worried or anything. Very calmly she told me she was popping along to Rosie Inkpen and that I had to keep an eye on Buster for a couple of minutes.

Rosie Inkpen came in and stayed while Mum went out. She

was gone a long time, it seemed to me. Rosie was nice and tried to make me smile, and she stopped Buster from hollering by stroking his forehead and making him fall into a trance.

Mum came back with a strange man in a grey suit. He looked very important and slightly fat. Rosie stayed in the bedroom with the baby and Mum took the man and me into the living room. He looked into my eyes, moved my head from side to side, sat me on the dining table and got a little hammer out and banged my knees so hard that it made them flip upwards all on their own. Then he listened to my chest with a stethoscope. It reminded me of the time I had swallowed a silver sixpence and had to go to hospital and be spun round on the bed. They were all disappointed in me because I wouldn't be sick for them. For days I had to be a baby again and do number twos in the po. Nanny and Mum would investigate, till one day they found the sixpence and all was right with the world.

The doctor scooped me off the table and sent me in to Rosie while he talked to Mum. Rosie put Buster into his cot and went and listened at the door. I followed. I couldn't bend my head properly so I strained my ears.

'. . . some kind of palsy, Mrs Marney. Has she been frightened by anything? Is she a nervous girl, would you say?'

Mum spoke so quietly that I couldn't hear a thing.

And without a goodbye he was gone, Mum calling out her 'thank you very much'es a few too many times, I thought.

No school for the rest of the week. I was given boiled eggs and mashed potato to eat because I couldn't chew properly without biting the inside of my mouth. I heard Mum tell Dad when he got home from work that she thought I'd had some kind of a stroke or that it was polio or something.

It went as mysteriously as it had arrived and I was back at school on the Monday.

*

Buster wasn't a baby, he was a bomb that had landed in my life. He could walk and talk by the time he was ten months old and he wanted to destroy everything. While I was at school Mum would have to strap him into his pram and place him in the passage with the front door open, so that she could get on with her chores and he had a chance to see the world. He was not a popular baby.

'Oi, Win! Come and see what he's doing.' The old lady from next door had ducked, luckily. Mum ran out and found that Buster had discovered the inside of his nappy and didn't like what he was sitting on. He would scoop out his poo and throw it as far as he could. He wasn't too difficult to potty-train after that.

I still did a four-day week at school, even though our Friday visits to Plaistow had stopped. Friday was maintenance day, followed by me looking after Buster while Mum went shopping for the weekend. Sometimes we all went, though she was nervous that the school-board man might spot us and she would get into trouble. Miss Coates, the headmistress at St Luke's, seemed to have come to some private arrangement with Mum over the Fridays, but we still mustn't let the school-board man find me.

Dad didn't see the point of me going, as the whole day was spent in St Luke's church for the weekly sermon and singing, back to school for playtime, then religious education until dinner time. In the afternoon we were allowed to read or draw. So it wasn't a proper school day.

'She's better off here, giving you a hand, than wasting her time hearing dog-collar fairy stories,' he said.

I had been told when I was little that Garwobs and God knew every move I made, every thought I thought. Garwobs had been Nanny's special agent.

'If you don't behave yourself, madam, Garwobs will come

and take you away, *for ever*. He's got one of his three eyes on you all the time.'

I always imagined Garwobs to look like Pat Jones, only more frightening. Everyone I knew called Pat 'Cyclops', and Mum had explained to me that the Cyclops had one eye in the middle of his head. I never mentioned it to Pattie because, after all, Pat Jones was her dad, I think.

We didn't have many visitors on the Isle of Dogs, but there were lots of letters, all to Mum. She knew the handwriting before she opened them.

Friday
20 April 1956

Dear Win,

Our Doll came and saw me today and told me your news. She also said that your Bill wasn't too happy about it. Well, there you are. He'll have to get used to it, won't he? You can't get knocked up on your own. What does he think, that he wasn't there? They make you laugh, don't they? Our Vi said she knew someone who could help you out, but after the last turn-out, when that woman died and everything, me and Doll knew it wasn't for you.

You've got our Rob to give you a hand, she's sensible enough.

If this one is due in September, your Buster will only be a couple of months off being two. So make sure he's clean by then. You can save all the baby stuff, which will come in handy. Won't have all that outlay this time.

I'm sure our Carol is carrying as well. She's only missed one period so far but she's already got that ripe look in her eye. Poor little cow.

Pattie got a postcard from Flo post-marked Lancashire. Doing what? Don't ask. Pat Jones comes to see Pattie regular as clockwork. Robert has given Carol's Galoot his cards, he's never going to make a plumber apparently. I don't suppose your Bill could put a word in with the asphalting, could he?

Why don't the lot of you come over on Sunday, in the afternoon. I do miss our Rob, you know. It's understandable, isn't it, Win? I mean, I did bring her up. She should come and stay with us, and Buster, of course, when you're confined with this new one. I'll have kids coming out of my earholes. Pattie's here to help me. Mind you, she's just as dozy as her mother, isn't she? My George is running me ragged as ever, he's only got another twelve months at school and Robert says now that he's got rid of the Galoot he'll apprentice George, as long as he goes to night school. So hopefully that will keep him on the straight and narrow.

When you come on Sunday I should have the money to get your wedding ring out of pawn. I don't mind you telling Bill it was my fault.

Lots of love,

Mum.

'What's "knocked up", Mum?'

Mum was humpy with me. She was organizing herself to write a letter and decided to give me a talking to at the same time.

'Lesson one, Rob, never write your thoughts down on paper and send them – unless you can stick by what you've said, for ever. Lesson two, don't read other people's letters. You might read something about yourself that you don't like, and privacy is to be respected at all costs. Thirdly, never write on lined paper. Now, go on, get yourself off to school.'

I did the wall business along the landing, down the stairs, then I found I could manage the rest of the trip to school without the need for brick comfort. I was nearly nine years old. My head was healing up.

*

Oh, Mum, what a cock-up. You drummed it into me … never believe … don't trust the bastards … think for yourself … Dad would say the same.

Here we are: you, dead at sixty-seven years old, flat on your back with your stiff mouth wide open, yearning for a life, and me calling for you to wake up. Wake up, for fuck's sake, and don't leave me like this.

Four hours earlier I hadn't believed you: you had a cold – a *cold*. Why were you play-acting like this, talking gibberish? It was my turn to say, 'Eat something.' I'd bullied you to keep your own counsel and not blame Buster for upsetting Aunt Doll. Aunt Doll had known for years that her Ron was gay; it didn't need Buster's innocent – yes, Mum, innocent – remark to fly this way and that.

I treated you the way you had always treated me, and you died and I lived.

Wake up, Mum.

Wake up, Rob.

I had another brother and I was grateful for him. He was quiet and loving and not spoilt by Dad like Buster was. Buster talked all the time, asked questions all the time, ran round creating havoc. Nanny didn't take to him and I was jealous of him. Every time Dad said, 'Look at him, Win, he's a fucking genius. Look what he's up to now,' I thought, 'No one has ever said that about me.' Even when I was the first in my class to move on to library books after *Janet and John*, no one said 'Well done.' Mum and Dad had said, 'I don't suppose there's much competition at that school. Take the plates out, there's a good girl.' Mr Merrick, my teacher, made me feel special because he told the whole class and I was called to the front and told I could choose any book I wanted from the bookshelf. I took *Black Beauty*. I was very surprised it was about a horse,

I'd thought it might be about Uncle Korim and the Lascars.

'In the beginning was the Word . . .' I'd sit on Granddad's knee reading the Bible to him while Mum and Nanny would be whispering in the kitchen. He would hold the book and I'd cuddle baby Lionel. Buster would be taken out by Pattie to try and exhaust him. Dad would go upstairs and talk with Carol and the Galoot.

The whisperings and the Bible reading would be interrupted by knocks on the door signalling the arrival of the other aunts and their broods. George would be in and out, making his sisters laugh. He wouldn't sit down to eat anything and, when my mum asked him to, always said, 'It's all right, Win, I've just had something round me mate's house.'

Aunts and cousins swarmed in; Aunt Doll shouted to Uncle Len to make sure he'd put the brake on his car. He'd forgotten to do it once and nearly killed the milkman. Aunt Doll never let him forget it. When Aunt Vi heard about it she said: 'You silly sod, what did you warn him for? You could have got away without paying your milk bill.'

Every Boxing Day was the same. The only people missing were Uncle Robert and his wife, and often Aunt Flo. Pattie never talked to me about her mum. She talked instead of her dream of being a grown-up. She was going to marry a nice quiet man, hopefully looking a bit like Cliff Richard, and she was going to have a nice house and two babies. Cousin Ron passed me a note one Sunday as they were leaving. It said: 'Found out that Black Gary's mum is really Aunt Flo and not Aunt Vi. Ask Pattie.'

I looked at Pattie and I looked at Gary. I decided to wait – not today. I needed to plot this out and pounce while her mouth was still open. The family motto was inbred in me, I'd heard variations on it all my life: 'Don't you worry, I'll bide my time and when they least expect it I'll get to the bottom of it.'

My aunts couldn't wait, though. In their different ways they would jump the gun and expose themselves. Nanny had the patience and sleight of hand.

If someone upset Aunt Vi, she would leap like a cat, swearing, throwing things, and finally exposing someone's secret. Lashing out to hurt anyone but herself.

Aunt Doll would try to be stately – wait it out – but her stony face would give her away. When she found she was getting nowhere she'd put her coat on and say, 'Pull yourself down, Mum, I'm not coming with you. All right?'

My mum had her own version. She would survey whatever emotional devastation had occurred, ask outright why she was being fucked about like this and lied to, and then go and look out of the window. As the years went by, her resolve grew more powerful that one day, one day, she would be free of this family.

I watched these women.

When Aunt Flo was around she had to stay at home with us kids and make sure we behaved ourselves while the others had a night down the pub.

We didn't.

It was Big George's idea and it was funny and frightening. By the time the grown-ups had left, the babies were asleep in the beds upstairs in Carol's part of the house. Pattie had to stay up there with them in case they woke up. Downstairs, Aunt Flo didn't stand much of a chance of keeping the rest of us in order.

The two Georges were the ringleaders. There was a box of Babycham and a crate of stout out in the scullery. Big George was planning an assault on his sister Flo. He got us to play noisy war games, diving through the passage, shrieking and hollering until we all got hysterical and the babies upstairs woke up and started crying. Flo held her head with the noise and confusion and ran upstairs to quieten them down.

We turned the lights off and hid in various corners – under Nanny's bed, under the dining table, in the meter cupboard under the stairs – and when Flo came back down she had a new fright. We could hear her searching for a light switch, thinking she had imagined everyone there. Then she heard stifled giggling coming from all corners of the damp, dark basement.

Big George in the meter cupboard was out first and we followed with the noisiest 'Whoooooooooooooooooooo' we could make.

Ron and me thought Flo was going to collapse. She started to howl with fear and was as white as the sheet that Little George had over his head. I had frightened myself with my 'Whoooooooooo'-ing because I hated the dark, though I kept quiet about it so that no one would play these tricks on me. I turned the lights on as soon as I could find them.

I thought Flo was going to die.

Her eyes rolled into her head and disappeared, her body got taller and went very stiff, she started making choking sounds and white bubbles foamed out of her mouth. She fell on the floor, with her back arching, still making gurgling noises. We stared at her in silence. Ron and I looked at Black Gary and wondered if he knew that this horror film on the floor was his real mum.

As soon as we had heard the merry grown-ups returning from the pub, we had all pretended to be asleep. We left Aunt Flo to her fate. After a lot of shouting and hollering she was sent to bed.

'The old man's lost his teeth. Anyone seen them?' Nanny was shouting.

Every morning after a pub night was the same.

'Did you lose them down the lav, Dad?' Aunt Doll called out.

'You sure you took them out with you?' asked Aunt Vi.

'They're his teeth, Vi, not a fucking pair of gloves,' snapped Nanny.

★

It was Sunday. I was sitting out the front of the flats so that Mum could see us at all times from the landing, keeping an eye on my two brothers.

Vicky Hawkins had just marched past, arm in arm with Ann Flood. They had both got into the Catholic grammar school and I was now a complete nothing because I had failed my eleven-plus and had to go to the local secondary modern in Limehouse.

It was a summer Sunday. Dinner was over and Dad was having his afternoon nap while Mum washed up. We had a few hours to play before our winkles and cockles. Other kids were around, on roller skates, playing hopscotch, and I was juggling, trying to keep three balls in the air.

Then everything went quiet. We all looked in the same direction. There, in the bright light of a Sunday afternoon, were Aunt Vi, Black Gary, and coffee-coloured Little George. They didn't visit us that often, and when they did it was when it was dark. Behind them was a black man I'd never seen before: Fahir, Uncle Korim's brother, newly arrived from an Indian village.

'Hello, darling, and what are you up to?' asked Aunt Vi.

All eyes were on me. I stared at my family and fell inside myself with shame. I could hear the whispers: 'They're black, she knows black people.' I ran upstairs, leaving my brothers, my aunt, my cousins behind me.

The only black people seen on the Isle of Dogs came from the ships and they didn't stay around for long.

I locked myself in the lavatory to work out some kind of strategy. I heard them arrive and Mum sounded surprised and curious. Dad woke up. I heard Mum go outside and look for us over the landing.

I knew she would discover the boys downstairs on their own. I didn't want to go back down there for all the other kids to take the mickey out of me.

'Where's our Rob?' she shouted down to Buster.

'I'm in the lav,' I shouted back.

She flew down the stairs. I stayed in there as long as I could, but was interrupted by a bang on the door. This new black man in our lives wanted to use it.

We brushed against each other as I tried to get out and he tried to get in. His hand moved to my beginnings of a bumpy breast and squeezed.

'What did you think you were doing, leaving the boys down there on their own? You're supposed to look after them. If you need a wee then you bring them up here with you. How many more times?' Mum nagged.

I put my hands over my ears and went to put the kettle on for our visitors. I wanted to be left alone for a while.

He had touched me – where he shouldn't.

I stared at the steam bubbling out of the kettle and imagined all the kids downstairs laughing about my black family. I imagined they had seen this black man squeeze my chest and that I was now down there with them with no clothes on and there was no escape.

I jumped out of my skin. There was someone behind me.

It was Black Gary, come to help me with the tea things.

He always looked as if he was about to cry. Aunt Vi was for ever moaning about how lazy he was, how stupid, how grubby – just like his mother.

I wanted to throw my ache off and hit him with it. I eyeballed him and worked out a speech in my head, shaping the words spitefully: 'You're not Aunt Vi's son, do you know that?'

It was as if he didn't hear me. Had I said it aloud?

He poured the hot water in the teapot and looked around for where the cups might be.

'Dozy Flo is your real mum. Dozy, dozy Flo,' I whispered in his ear.

'I know,' was all he said, and I learned that doing something like that didn't make me feel any better.

Mum knew that something was up with me because she always watched us like a hawk. At first she thought it was because of the bollocking she'd given me. Aunt Vi and her troop left pretty soon after we'd finished our tea. The new black man hadn't eaten any; he'd sat and smoked strange, blue-coloured fags. As Mum closed the street door on them, I ran to the lav and made it just in time. I sicked up my tea and sat sweating on the floor. She thought I had winkle poisoning, put me to bed, gave me some white butcher's paper and pencils, and told me I mustn't lie down because if I was sick again I might die. If only. Mum kept checking up on me and after a few hours it dawned on her that I hadn't been poisoned at all.

'What's up? Come on, Rob, you've been a funny girl all afternoon. You didn't say a word to Aunt Vi and I think she was a bit hurt by it. Has someone said somthing?'

I shook my head and carried on writing rhyming words.

Light as a feather.

Hang by leather.

Terrible weather.

Never.

Ever.

Sever.

Whack.

Black.

Jack.

She took away the pencil and made me look at her. 'Did he come into the lav when you were in there?'

'No, I was already finished,' I said.

She got it out of me in the end. I kept saying it was probably a mistake, that he hadn't meant to do it. She closed her face in preparation for war.

Dear Vi,

What you do with your life, or who you hang about with, has never been any concern of mine. Until it affects me, that is. You say this Fahir you brought over to us uninvited yesterday is Korim's brother – that may very well be the case, but don't you ever bring him near me or mine again. My Bill will knock his fucking liver and lights out – that's if I don't get there first. You wondered why my Rob was quiet? Well your ever-so-friendly native got a bit too friendly with a twelve-year-old kid. Need I say more? I don't think so.

Win.

That set the cat among the pigeons. Three days later Uncle Len and Aunt Doll brought Nanny over. I was sent to bed but still managed to hear most of it. There were lots of 'He reckons she imagined it' . . . 'She's at that age, isn't she?' . . . 'Win, you've really upset Vi over this' . . .

Dad and Uncle Len were sent to the pub, and by the sound of it they were more than happy to go.

'Let me speak to her,' I heard Nanny say.

'I'm not having you put words into her mouth so you can justify staying in with Vi. You know it's wrong as well as I do. I knew he was a shifty bastard the minute I clapped eyes on him.' Mum was getting really upset now.

Then a big row started about how Vi could do no wrong and that she had always been Nanny's favourite – that Nanny and Vi were two of a kind. Aunt Doll told Mum not to upset herself.

'Oh, right, Doll. If this happened to your Barbara, who would you believe, eh? Some lazy bastard Indian or her?' That shut them up.

I hid under the covers and thought about going in and saying sorry, that I had made it all up for a joke, anything to stop the shouting.

Aunt Doll came in to me. She smelt of flowers and lipstick

and was wearing a blue-flowered summer frock with a little pink cardigan over it. She pulled back the covers and hugged me to her big warm fleshy bosom.

'Now, Rob, you take no notice of what they're saying in there. What they're going on about is of no importance. What is very important is if anyone has taken liberties with my god-daughter. You can tell me anything you like. Tell me from the very beginning what happened.'

I juggled with the two voices in my head. Number one was saying that it would be easier to say I made a mistake. Number two was pushing for the truth.

'I think at first it was a mistake, that he didn't mean to do it, then when his hand did touch me he squeezed me hard and it hurt.'

She looked at me, kissed the top of my head, grabbed my hand and said, 'Come on, come and see your poor old nan.'

Mum took me off Aunt Doll as if I were going to be kidnapped, and Nanny shook her head and looked really fed up with me.

Then she rummaged in her shopping bag. Out came the present she had been promising me for about two years: a tin globe of the world with a light-blue base and hinge.

I felt guilty and mean, and she knew it. I felt guilty for telling the truth. I was learning. Never say more than you have to about important private thoughts. Don't say it, don't write it down, keep your own counsel, and keep watching.

The next day Aunt Doll visited Aunt Vi. Ten minutes later Fahir walked in. Aunt Vi didn't say a word to him; she punched him in the face so hard that he lost his footing and two teeth.

We didn't see Nanny and Granddad or Aunt Vi for months. No one spoke of them. Mum would go to the call box by the post office every Friday and ring Aunt Doll to check that all was well.

This Friday it wasn't. Nanny had been taken to hospital, she would be staying for at least ten days. She was only sixty and, although she didn't know it, she had another twenty-six years ahead of her.

'Malnutrition? Where did she dig that word up from? She's too fat anyway.' I heard Mum say.

I wanted us to go and visit her, but Mum was having none of it. Aunt Doll went every day. At the end of the first week we went over to cook Granddad a Sunday roast. All the family turned up, but Aunt Vi didn't bring Fahir with her.

'Every day I've been in I've said hello to this old lady opposite Mum. Well, this morning the old lady was fast asleep, so I didn't disturb her. Me and Mum are chatting away, but I can't help looking at the old girl opposite, then Mum says, "What do you keep looking over there for?" and I says, "I think that old lady has died, Mum." Do you know what she says? "Who the fuck have you come to visit? Her or me?"'

Aunt Doll made everyone laugh, apart from Granddad, who said, 'She's got a point, Doll.'

Nanny's malnutrition went away and she was ordered not to live on Rich Tea biscuits anymore, and she must have at least one good meal a day. She lived, but soon afterwards Uncle Korim died and Aunt Vi married Fahir –or so she said, nobody witnessed it.

Uncle Korim's funeral was very strange, apparently. Nanny, Aunt Doll, and Carol went, and they told Mum that it was a good turn-out – about two hundred people, mainly Indians – and everyone, including our lot, had to walk along with large black umbrellas open as if it were raining. It was a long walk.

We were all growing up and life was spent almost entirely on the Isle of Dogs and Plaistow was featuring less and less. It was such a slow process that I didn't notice.

I thought that Nanny's visits to us were about seeing me. If it was late she would insist that Mum get me out of bed so she could give me a kiss and ask about school. Then she would cry about something and we knew what was coming. She owed money and was going to have to go to court. With grim faces all round, Dad would insist that Nanny should have whatever money was in the house, and in the morning Mum would have to pawn her wedding ring to see the rest of us through the week. Off Nanny would trot with a grateful 'What would I do without you, Win? I'd never come between you and Bill if I could help it. I promise you'll get it back next week.'

'You fall for it every time, Bill, don't you. She's fucking Oscar-winning. Let her go to court and weave her sob story round the judge. I've just about had enough of the lot of you. She uses my Rob to get round all of us.' Mum would sound as tough as she could, batting away the constant haunting of defeat. Dad would look confused and go to bed.

Nanny stopped coming and Mum stopped visiting her.

Big George had been coming to stay with us most weekends for years, while he was saving up to get married and even after he was married. Mum and Aunt Doll wrote to each other every week, and during the summer we would make the occasional trip to see her where the Harrises went camping, at Grange Farm down in Essex. We never ever saw Uncle Robert, so he wasn't missed. Aunt Vi, Aunt Flo, and even Carol were being kept at a greater distance now. This was the way Mum wanted it, but she couldn't be parted from Big George or Doll, just as I couldn't part with Nanny and Granddad. Every now and again I would be allowed to visit them on my own on a Sunday afternoon, paying my own fare out of the baby-sitting money that I'd earned from the neighbour downstairs.

'I want you back home by half past four. Don't you be late or you'll put years on me. And make sure she doesn't get any money out of you. Don't you feel sorry for her, because it's all lies,' Mum would say.

I always came home penniless and was given the third degree.

'Aunt Flo came back and left these two kids with Nanny. She said she had to delouse them. Aunt Flo disappeared again, so Nanny is going to take them down the council home tomorrow morning,' I said.

'That's what she tried to do with you when you were born. Don't get it into your head that she thinks the world of you because she doesn't.'

Mum knew that she had said more than she should have done. If she had said any more I would have known the secret we both carried around with us. I wasn't sure what it was, but I did know that it had to with the 'before' man, the bus conductor. If ever I got on his bus on my own, he wouldn't look at me; he would pass me by and pretend not see me trying to pay the fare. I never told Mum this happened.

Mum had little jobs, early-morning cleaning down at the Tooke Arms, which she could finish before we went off to school, and in a cake factory in the evening. She had a running-away glint in her eye. She was thirty-five and all her kids were at school. I had never been allowed out on my own unless I had the two boys with me, and by fourteen I had that same glint. One more year at school and I would be free.

What was she dreaming of? What was I dreaming of?

Only today came with a guarantee.

It was so hot that September – steamy, sticky, smelly city weather. I had two weeks to go. Walking to the bus stop I thought of my dreams, of being a barrister – silly cow, I had failed my eleven-plus – of being a dress-designer – but I couldn't sew.

'You will not do factory work, of that I'm determined,' Mum had said. So here I was, an ex-dental nurse working as a telephonist. I had imagined that being a dental nurse might one day have turned me into a dentist. It wasn't all bad. I loved plugging in to hidden people's conversations; I saw myself as if in a movie, being important, the link between the dialling tone and the human voice. No one on the other end had any idea what I looked like, who I was. I had become the bits between the bricks. I was eighteen years old and still in love with the wall.

The bus was jam-packed; people squirmed and nudged to find the last standing places. I gave the conductor my fare and he took it. I slipped him a short, curved look, took a deep breath, and he moved on.

'In about two weeks I will give birth to this bus conductor's grandchild. He … took my fare.' I didn't say it, though, didn't say a dicky bird.

I hung on to the strap with one hand and ate the bus ticket.

No one offered me a seat.

Acknowledgements

I would like to thank Miriam Segal for getting me into this fine mess; Toby Mundy for twisting my arm; Claire Paterson for spoiling me; Fidelis Morgan for her detective work; Peter Guinness for having the patience of a saint; my friends and family for allowing me to disappear for two years; and finally to Dr Louisa Joyner for her brilliant editorship, laughs, meals and booze.